Symbols of Power in Philosophy

What the great minds of our past have to teach us about today's issues

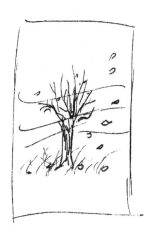

By Mathias Karayan
Copyright 2015
All rights reserved

www.karayanpublishing.com

Cover design: Francesca Suzio

Layout: Trina Koning

Library of Congress Control Number
2015904359

ISBN: 978-0-9820675-2-9

This book can be purchased at:
BUFFALO BOOKS & COFFEE
6 Division Street
Buffalo, MN 55313
763-682-3147

Other books by *Mathias Karayan*

Healing the Wound: The Family's Journey through Chemical Dependency
*
The Way Home: Stories from the Master
*
Symbols of Power (in Metaphysics)

Available at *www.karayanpublishing.com*

The Edge of Passage Series

To start your journey involves the conviction that *there is more to living than what your world offers.* The desire to want to step beyond this view is to start your journey home. As you begin to recognize your time as a passing through, being a passerby, you begin to understand the messages of what people and events are really about. This is what *The Edge of Passage Series* is about. Wherever you go you take yourself with you. Are you ready?

The first book in the series; *The Way Home; Stories from the Master,* deals with the paradoxical experience of living life on life's terms.

The second book in the series; *Symbols of Power* (in Metaphysics) addresses the experience of brushing up against the veil; life from the other side. Most all of us have had these experiences but have also dismissed them as fanciful or strange.

This current book, *Symbols of Power in Philosophy* is the third book in *The Edge of Passage Series.* This book discusses what the great minds of the past have to teach us about today's issues.

All things are wearisome
Man is not able to tell it
The eye is not satisfied with seeing
Nor is the ear filled with hearing
That which has been is that which will be
And that which has been done
Is that which will be done
So, there is nothing new under the sun

The Preacher
Ecclesiastes 1:9-10[1]

---

[1] Unless otherwise stated, all biblical quotes that follow are out of the New American Standard Version (NASV).

Contents

Symbols of Power in Philosophy

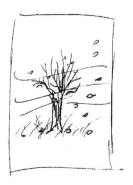

Foreword: A Personal Note

Some of us are digging in
Some of us are holding our own
Some of us are digging out
All I'm doing is leaving a paper trail

Looking back on my life, and given my experience of moving through religious thinking, I was moving towards being an Existential Taoist Pagan. Are those three compatible? Probably not, but they do reflect the best way to explain the complexity of my world as I once viewed it.

The Taoist
As a kid growing up, I loved to play. There was nothing else. Therefore, I could never quite buy into what was going on around me. Deep in my being I felt there was something that was not right and I could not put my finger on it. Looking at who I thought God was as viewed through religious beliefs and practices, I came to think that either God was crazy or religion got it wrong. To make a long story short, I was raised Catholic. In the early 1970's, I was a wanderer who hitch-hiked all over the country. At the time I did not consider myself to be a "hippie." However, looking back, I lived that lifestyle.

From the mid to late 70's, I tried to take on the beliefs, experience and education[2] of a fundamental evangelical view.[3] I became softened to look beyond it through a

---

[2] My BA is in Biblical Theology.
[3] Evangelicalism is a movement in modern Anglo-American

liberation theology view.[4] At the same time I became a voracious reader of philosophical thought.

Eventually, I could not reconcile the paradox of a God who created a world to tempt humans to sin so He could throw them out of a paradise He made for them, to suffer birth, pain and death. And a God who is Omniscient[5] allows his perfect creation to suffer made no sense. And there are people from each side of the battle line who justify the killing of each other, "With God on Our Side"[6] is true madness. Then there are those who try to justify an insane ideology that says God created an earth that hurts and kills the innocent and evil alike. It also made no sense that we were born into a world of *choice* with no choice but to sin then die. And what *choice* do I have but to continue to mess up God's creation when it was handed down to me by my heirs, already messed up?[7] I could not bring myself to believe in a psycho God who saw his creation as "very good."[8]

Protestantism that emphasizes personal commitment to Christ and the authority of the Bible.

[4] Liberation Theology emphasizes the teachings of Christ that address the issues of social and economic justice for the oppressed.

[5] All knowing

[6] Bob Dylan (1941-) is an American musician and prolific songwriter who is one of the most important figures in contemporary folk and rock music.

[7] Genesis 3:16-19; Romans 8: 20-22

[8] Genesis 1:31

Eventually, I became attracted to a Taoist understanding of how the world works. What made sense was Lao-tzu's[9] riddle:

The Tao is like a well: used but never used up
It is like the eternal void: filled with infinite possibilities
It is hidden but always present
I don't know who gave birth to it
It is older than God

Tao Te Ching #4[10]

The Existentialist

From the late 1970's into the 1980's I was attracted to philosophical readings; especially to the writings of Søren Kierkegaard[11] who railed against a lukewarm Danish Lutheran church and the rational Hegelian philosophy[12]

---

[9] Nothing is known about Lao-tzu. He may have been an older contemporary of Confucius (551-479 BC). True to his writings, Lao-tzu left no trace but the Tao Te Ching (usually pronounced Dow Deh Jing). Among other things, whether it is about a child or a country, his book is a treatise on the art of governing. The Tao is an excellent study in duality, balance and centering. It is one of the most influential books in our history.

[10] All translations by Stephen Mitchell

[11] Søren Aabye Kierkegaard (1813-1855) was a Danish religious philosopher who focused on individual existence, choice, and commitment. His writings influenced modern theology and philosophy. I consider him to be the father of modern existentialism. Because he is unsystematic in his writings, to read him can be exasperating, until you get to know him.

[12] Georg Wilhelm Friedrich Hegel (1770-1831) was a German

of the day. Hegel taught that human kind was moving through an impersonal dialectical process[13] of conflict resolution that achieved a higher truth. In response, Kierkegaard wrote that it was a decision of *the individual* to step out with courage, "a Leap of Faith"[14] to be authentic in the midst of life that presented itself as an unpredictable contradiction.

A step further along my existential way was the writings of Friedrich Wilhelm Nietzsche[15] who wrote about "Das Übermensch,"[16] a superman when released of the shackles of traditional ethics and morality embodied the best qualities of the creative individual. According to Nietzsche, this man was the highest expression of the "will to power," the force that produces all human accomplishments.[17]

---

philosopher who saw all actions and reactions as the movement of resolution towards pure thought (the absolute principle or God).

[13] Thesis – antithesis resolving to synthesis

[14] Kierkegaard's book; *Fear and Trembling*

[15] Friedrich Wilhelm Nietzsche (1844-1900) was a German philosopher, poet, and classical philologist who, as one of the most provocative thinkers of the 19th century, is still provocative today.

[16] Nietzsche's books; *Thus Spoke Zarathustra* & *The Will to Power*

[17] The Nazi and Fascist movements of the 1920's took Nietzsche out of context for purposes of exploitation. But then again, what can't be taken out of context for purposes of defending an ideology of self-deception?

The Pagan[18]

In the early 1980's, while living in, working with, and being a part of the Native American community, I became interested in the writings of Baruch Spinoza.[19] Spinoza asserted that the universe is identical with God, who is the uncaused "substance" of all things. Along with my natural love for nature, the outdoors, the changing of the seasons, I could avoid an agnostic/atheistic dilemma. I could still believe in God and nature could be my god and goddess. The pagan part of me was coming to a conclusion that the only thing that made sense, worth honoring or loving in this world of religious, political, ethical and economic madness was the beauty of ever-changing nature. To quote an overused platitude: "The only thing absolute is change."

Seeing nature as an inspiration naturally brought out the environmentalist in me. It was only a matter of simple common sense to see that the only sane thing to do was to stop the insanity of minds bent on destroying the earth as a means for body comfort when the body needs the earth for survival. I was becoming a true skeptic.[20]

---

[18] Historically, paganism has been identified as the worship of many gods. Currently, most pagans believe in the divine character of the natural world where Paganism is often described as an "Earth religion," that divinity is found in mind and nature.

[19] Baruch Spinoza (1632-1677) was a Dutch rationalist philosopher and religious thinker, regarded as the most modern exponent of pantheism.

[20] Skepticism in philosophy is the doctrine that denies the possibility of attaining knowledge of reality as it is in itself, apart from human perception.

Rapture Beyond Belief

However, beyond my body of understanding[21] and unpredictable to my conscious mind, in January of 1984, I was raptured out of my current experience.[22] I was sitting comfortably reading a book by Gerald G. Jampolsky titled *Teach Only Love*. I came to a passage that read:

> *To be free of conflict requires only one thing: A goal that is not itself conflicted. Trying to change anything is a form of battle; wanting something that can only be ours in the future is to block our potential to be happy now. Therefore, set for yourself a goal that can be fulfilled where you stand. Make this instant your door to freedom and you will find that it will crack open a little further each time you return to this moment in peace.*

Following through with what the words suggested, rather than my propensity to want a conflicted goal or a future goal or to want to change something, my mind naturally asked for an undivided goal; peace of mind. What followed was the surprise of an overwhelmingly indescribable joy. For an hour of eternity, I laid with my back on the floor experiencing tears of joy. For a number of days that followed, I was at peace with myself and with the world. I was free of all fear; and when I returned to my "so-called" body experience, I could not view anything

---

[21] Beyond my ideology/paradigm/set of organized beliefs
[22] My brush against the veil of the other side; in the foreword of my book, *The Way Home*

as I had before. I was forever changed and I could not look back. I could not un-ring the bell.[23]

Synthesis

In a Kierkegaardian sense I came to the understanding that not only does life present itself as confusing contradictions, but I have a responsibility, a decision to walk with courage through the confusing fears of life's contradictions. If I look for it, there is always a door for me to open. I can't know what is on the other side of the door until I find the courage to walk through my fear -- "a leap of faith."

In a Nietzschian sense the world shows me over and over again that it is not a "will to power" by which I authenticate my individual self. That just breeds the opportunity for opposition and opposition begets conflict and conflict magnified makes the world a battleground. The world from the beginning of written record has been a battleground of wills for power. Rather, I found in the "will to love" the power of a peace that transcends the will to power this world offers.

My decision to awaken ...
Is in direct relation to my will to love
Since all healing involves replacing fear with love

---

[23] From this point on in my life I realized that I could not be purely objective. But then, I never met anyone who was purely objective. I readily admit that I am continually tempted to presume too much. *The Way Home; p53*

A Unifying Goal

For me, my journey to peace of mind has been the only unifying goal that makes sense for a confused mind. Glimpses of the goal are the experiences that feed me along the way. Faith was needed in the beginning but it was the overwhelming experience of "peace" itself that feeds me and transcends the need for "a leap of faith."

The only means to peace is through peace itself

Aware of my bias, I can proceed more honestly through the history of philosophical thinking with the luxury of presenting the diverse views of some of the greatest minds of our history. *Generally* speaking, regarding living life with purpose and meaning, the question for the content of this book is: **What does the discipline of philosophy have to teach us? What does the data suggest?** *Specifically*, you will find what follows to be organized topically and yet somewhat unsystematic.

Mathias Karayan
September 2015

Life's but a walking shadow, a poor player that struts and frets his hour upon the stage, and then is heard no more; it is a tale told by an idiot, full of sound and fury, signifying nothing.

William Shakespeare

Symbols of Power in Philosophy

Introduction:
Philosophy's Role for Today

To derive "meaning" always makes the observer a participant

Introduction

Every living being has the same basic wish – to be happy and to avoid suffering. Even newborn babies, animals, and insects have this wish. It has been our main wish since beginning-less time and it is with us all the time, even during our sleep. We spend our whole life working hard to fulfill this wish.

Buddha[24]

The traditional question often asked over the history of time in a philosophical[25] way has been, *"What is the meaning of life?"* More specifically, in a physical world

---

[24] The Buddha who is the founder of the Buddhist religion is called Buddha Shakyamuni. "Shakya" is the name of the royal family into which he was born and "Muni" means "Able One." Buddha Shakyamuni was born as a royal prince in 624 BC in a place called Lumbini, in what is now Nepal. In general, 'Buddha' means 'Awakened One', someone who has awakened from the sleep of ignorance and sees things as they really are.

[25] The word philosophy is from the Greek meaning "love of wisdom." *Philo* is one of the Greek words for love and *Sophia* is the Greek word for wisdom. A philosopher is one who loves or searches for wisdom.

that is ever-changing Martin Heidegger[26] asks what he considered the essential philosophical question: *What is it to be?* Said another way, and given your interaction between your inner world and the outer world,[27] *"What is my bliss?"*[28] In one form or another, these statements have been the center of philosophical discussion since the dawn of this civilization.

Because the above statements involve a desire to want to know, they reflect the idea that you lack completion. They also presume that human kind is motivated to be happy and that the means to happiness can be achieved through "knowledge."[29] Psychologically speaking, this process can be called self-actualizing. Blocks to self-actualizing towards happiness would be called ignorance. Resistance to want to know would be denial. Mental

---

[26] Martin Heidegger (1889-1976) was a German philosopher who developed existential phenomenology and is widely regarded as the most original and influential 20th-century philosopher.

[27] The inner world as a knowing from within, other than sense experience; the outer world as knowing being derived from the sensations and perceptions of the world (empiricism). Epistemology is the study of "how" knowledge is derived. Can knowing be derived from sense experience? Is there anything to know beyond sense experience?

[28] Aristotle (384-322 BC) was a Greek philosopher and scientist. Aristotle, Plato's pupil, regarded happiness as the aim of life.

[29] Socrates (469-399BC) was a Greek philosopher who believed people were not willfully bad, just self-defeating out of ignorance. People were motivated to be happy through knowledge. Socrates greatly affected Western philosophy through his influence on Plato.

illness is the state of mind dealing with a physiological disposition that involves ignorance and denial. As it seems, we all have a dance to play between mind and body.

The Paper Trail

The question *"What is my bliss?"* infers the next question: *"How do I get there?"* Obvious and simple answers to that question are easily provided. "Just be" or "Be in the moment" or "Let go and let God" or "It is what it is" are a few of the many intellectual platitudes. I do not deny that these comments may be relevant to the question at hand. But it can be the service of philosophical consideration that provides a paper trail to the experience of what your bliss is rather than trite intellectual platitudes.

My journey is experience based. The academics of those who have gone before us is a paper trail we can use.

Life's speculation is a dance between your inner and outer world that philosophy often divides into four main branches; *metaphysics*,[30] the investigation of ultimate reality; *epistemology*, the study of the origins, validity, and limits of knowledge; *ethics,* the study of the nature of morality and judgment; and *aesthetics*, the study of the nature of beauty in the fine arts.

More recently, philosophical speculation has included *analytic philosophy,* which assumes that careful analysis

---

[30] Metaphysics is the topic of conversation in my previous book entitled *Symbols of Power.*

of language and concepts can clear up problems and confusions concerning issues in the history of philosophy that became meaningless because philosophers misunderstood or misused philosophical language. Analytically speaking, the use of words that ask what is "practical" and "relevant" are terms in a context that involve the realm of "personal" interpretation. This is the language of philosophical speculation in all its glory. As I already stated, *to derive "meaning" always makes the observer a participant.* And the semantics of analytical philosophy makes everyone a philosopher.

Philosophical Speculation as a Process

You may argue that the realm of philosophical speculation is not practical or relevant to the everyday living of our age. Reduce this speculation to the arena of intellectual bantering and your argument is justified. However, any mind that asks *"What is my bliss?"* in some fashion or form[31] is a mind involved in philosophical speculation. No matter how hard you may want to deny it, everyone has a view of life that is speculative as to what the dance between your inner and outer world means.

You may argue that what was just stated is but a matter of semantics. You are right. But tell me, what does not involve semantics[32] in the area of communicating life's meaning? Therefore, *philosophical speculation is the process of understanding your existence as a statement of personal meaning between your inner and outer world.* Its

---

[31] Like the form of money, status, appearance, power, drugs, sex, relationship, accumulation, etc., to name a few.

[32] The study of how meaning in language is created; metaphor

reason is to find out specifically *"What is my bliss?"* Tied inextricably to that question is the broader question: *What does the discipline of philosophy have to teach us?*

The Focus

Said in many ways, the central philosophical discussion throughout the dawn of this civilization has been *"What is my bliss?"* This book is focused on the understanding of your existence (being) as a statement of personal meaning between your inner and outer world. This book's reason is to find out specifically *"What my bliss is."*

My Approach

This book's reason is not exhaustive in its approach to philosophical topics, nor is it strictly empirical. However, based on the observation of the samples presented,[33] this book does ask in an empirical way *"What does the data suggest?"*

The question "W*hat is my bliss?"* is an implied motivator that begs for the next question; *"Where is my bliss to be found?"*[34] By asking from the topic at hand *"What does the data suggest?"* **my approach** will be to negate the data irrelevant[35] to the question *"Where is my bliss to be found?"* In other words, as regards to the topic at hand, *"Can my bliss be found here?"* Negating the irrelevant allows for what is relevant to be self-revealing.[36]

---

[33] The topics presented are significantly broad enough to represent the field of philosophy.

[34] Also relevant to the question "What is my bliss?" is the question *"How do I get there?"*

[35] That which is immaterial or beside the point; mindless distractions

Is there a complication of data that makes it difficult to see its nothingness? We shall see what the data suggests. This search through the discipline of philosophy will obviously deal with the question; *what does the discipline called philosophy have to teach us?*

This book is about generalizing these questions to all forms the world of phenomena[37] presents. There is an explicit understanding that the observer asking questions is also a *participant* in the process of his observation of study. By no means do I pretend to be an objective observer. I have a point of view.[38] Because of my passion for philosophical speculation, it was primary for me to represent the diverse views clearly. Hopefully, I have

---

[36] This is not "a leap of faith" from the measure of quantitative data to the experience of qualitative meaning as much as it is a matter of getting out of the way to allow you to experience *"what already is."*

[37] Edmund Husserl (1859-1938) was a German philosopher, founder of phenomenology. He took Emanuel Kant's thoughts on "things in themselves" and our experience of "things in themselves" asserting that we cannot know anything directly because our experience of any object is different than the object itself. This makes the study of any object (the objective) irrelevant and the study of our experience of any object (the subjective) everything.

[38] Because of perception I have a point of view, you have a point of view; we all have an ideology of how we think the world works. To be able to move beyond *your ideology* is to first recognize that you have one. It is an assumption (usually hidden from our view) to help us operate in the world ... sometimes.

done this accurately. And with that said, *is there a complication of information that makes it difficult to see its nothingness?* Let's see what the data suggests. In the meantime;

Milk the cows of gladness, before they all go dry
Search the rim of madness, before you learn and sigh
Become a parch of dryness, before you stop to drink
Ascend the arch of whyness before you try to think

James Seals
Cows of Gladness

1. Topics of Conversation

An open mind has nothing to fear
A closed mind denies that it fears the truth

An open mind sees no past or future in anyone. Without worn out concepts to imprison the mind, it does not need to defend nor decide anything. Without intellectual clutter an open mind is free to look upon only what the present holds.

The truth of any present moment will show you the history of the whole world

A. Hypothetics:
The Language of Make-Believe

That which was ...
Are thoughts remembered ... in the present
That which may be ...
Are thoughts anticipating ... in the present
We live in a world of thoughts
Lost in a conditioned experience of tenses

Introduction

As previously noted, *analytic philosophy* assumes that careful examination of language and concepts can clear up problems and confusions concerning important issues in the history of philosophy. Used another way, analytical philosophy is the examination of language and concepts that reflect the interpretations of our world-views. What does the study of language via Hypothetics demonstrate? Let's take a look.

Hypothetics Defined

Simply stated, Hypothetics is the study of the language of tenses and its resulting experience. Hypothetics reflects the ideas of question and possibility. It is a quest to want to know beyond "what is." The language of Hypothetics can be postulated in three ways:

1. Empirical science uses hypothetical language or a hypothesis as a proposition for further investigation. For example, "Suppose we change a part of a child's curriculum. Would it make learning better?" With a

specific outcome defined and strict procedural rules for gathering data, information would be gathered for clarification, comparison, correlation and interpretation.

2. The language of Hypothetics also addresses a mind set on *future possibility.* "I can do it" is a statement regarding potential. "Can I do it?" is a question involving doubt. "What if it does or doesn't happen?" in all its forms is a statement that reflects anticipation and or anxiety. It is important to note that all of these statements are based on the present experience of a memory.

3. Hypothetics also addresses a mindset of *opportunity missed.* For example, the statement that "I should have" or "I should not have ..." reflects the outcome of a choice already made or missed. It is the perception of a present memory reflected as a past mistake, with future implications.

All three examples project a mindset of possibility unreal to the situation at hand. That is why Hypothetics is the language of make-believe.

For our investigation, we will focus on the third area of Hypothetics; your "opportunity missed."

Key Phrases
Phrases obvious to what you may see as your missed opportunity are:

"I should or shouldn't have ..."
"I could or couldn't have ..."
"If only I would or wouldn't have ..."
"Why did I or didn't I do that?"

These statements reflect personal responsibility for the idea of failure or opportunities missed. These statements also reflect a mindset of guilt and disappointment. Therefore, these statements reflect a mind that seeks resolution. Replacing the word "I" with the word "you" in the above phrases assumes responsibility somewhere else. They reflect a mindset of blame. The need to blame is a deflection away from not looking at your misinterpretations of life events.

There is nothing wrong about your excitement over possibility. But the idea of possibility so easily turns into your means for disappointment, guilt, hurt, and anger. Are you a frustrated learner because you seek resolution in a place it can't be found?

You might be able to consider hindsight to be your best friend ... if it wasn't your most ardent enemy

The Words You Use

Because an undisciplined mind is not proficient in resolution training ... hindsight is merciless to an undisciplined mind

The words you use reveal your inner world to those who are listening. In fact, *your investigation into hypothetical statements used by you will reveal a conspiracy of self-talk that you secretly plotted against yourself*

Because the above phrases betray disappointment, anger is not far behind. As a matter of fact disappointment is anger. The only difference is your choice of words. "You (or I) should have ..." are words that do not allow for acceptance. What words can you give that will appease anger's lack of acceptance? There is none. And as long as anger's acceptance is in the realm of the make-believe there will be no answer that will appease anger. But there is retaliation.

The language of an opportunity missed reveals your secret doubt, guilt, disappointment, anger and non-acceptance. Listen to the words you use. They display your belief in personal lack and thus incompletion. If it is the principle of your mind to find what it seeks, to say "I should have done it differently" is a mind that seeks punishment.

The Basic Tenses of Unreality

You experience your life "as if"
When you live through tenses that are not

Guilt, fond memories and resentment (anger held on to over time) are experienced as thoughts from the past. Hope, anxiety and fear are anticipation's of a future based on yesterday's memories. Do you want something to happen again? Do you want to avoid something that has or might happen?[39] You may think this is normal thinking, but it is how you have been conditioned to think and thus experience life. Your experience of life comes down to a mind unknowingly out of control, constantly reacting to its own interpretation of tenses that are not real. In other

---

[39] Every living being has the same basic wish; to be happy and to avoid suffering. Buddha

words, through denial you constantly sabotage the experience of resolution in the here and now.[40]

Don't let the past remind us of what we are not now

Stephen Stills

The Only Tense There Is

"What if" holds you hostage to the hypothetical

When it was yesterday, what tense were you in? Most people will say, "In the past." No, it was the present! When tomorrow arrives, what tense will you be in? The present! When are you not in the present? Never! Is it possible that you are constantly experiencing the thoughts of tenses that are not and denying yourself the experience of the only tense there is? As a matter of fact, experiencing the tenses of thought that are not real is what an illusion is; the experience of something that isn't. You will never find resolution in experiencing something that isn't. Look again. Is your mind more out of control than you realize?

Resolution Training

There's nowhere you can be that isn't where you're meant to be ... It's easy

Lennon & McCartney
All You Need Is Love

---

[40] *Symbols of Power p94*

Because you believe the way you see all your situations is the right way, you carry many messages that lack resolution. Do you need resolution training[41] that allows your mind to rest in the present?

Wherever you are right now is where you are supposed to be. How do you know this? Because that's where you are right now.[42] You may think this reasoning is overly simplistic; however, it is the ego that complicates nothingness. If you were able to think non–dualistically for a moment to suspend all judgment, this reasoning would clearly make perfect non-hypothetical sense. Does complicating the results of information make it difficult to see its nothingness?

Your mind is easily and anxiously tempted to think you "should" be somewhere else, doing something else. I assure you, you are where you are supposed to be right now! Disappointment and guilt says "If only I would have done this differently." Blame says "I should have done it differently." These comments are not problems out of failed opportunity. They are problems of thought, of accepting the mind-set of an undisciplined mind. When you think about being somewhere else or how things should have been different, you miss your lesson here and now.

---

[41] This training would be a disciplined focus of a unified goal that heals a mind split by dualistic (divided) hypothetical thinking.

[42] *The Way Home p184*

There's nothing you can say but you can learn how to play the game ... It's easy

Lennon & McCartney
All You Need Is Love

Summary

If it is the principle of your mind to find what it seeks, to say "I should have done it differently" is a mind that seeks punishment. Is reality yours to select?

"I wish I would have" is the guilt of an opportunity missed. You cannot change what happened. But isn't what happened nothing more than a parade of yesterday's memories? You will never change yesterday; but if you can change your interpretation of yesterday, then who needs to change yesterday? You can change the way you see what happened. Freedom from the chains of yesterday's meanings allows you the freedom to experience today free of guilt and look upon tomorrow from a different point of view.

There's nothing you can do but you can learn how to be you in time ... It's easy

Lennon & McCartney
All You Need Is Love

Because hypothetical thinking brings you into an experience of make believe, to negate hypothetical thinking leaves you with what? Allow your mind room to change so you can step towards the integration your mind holds for you to remember. Is reality yours to select or is there an experience of being ... beyond selection?

So, what does the study of language via Hypothetics demonstrate? To live within the tenses of the make-believe is to miss your opportunity to experience your completion in the only place where all tenses cease to exist; the eternal present.

> *What if there was guilt?*
> *What if there was loss?*
> *What if there was pain?*
> *We would have something we call a world*
>
> *Now, and just for a moment ...*
> *What if there was no world?*

B. The Concept of Duality

Knowledge does not involve the use of opposites
Perception does

Introduction

How you think about what you think about is your ideology
Transcendence is an experience beyond thought

In your mind there are two ways of looking at the world. When you look inside, the guide you choose for seeing will be the witness you behold looking out.[43] If you chose an ever-changing view, to have integrity of mind you will select only the witnesses that demonstrate your beliefs to be consistent with that view. You will discard the exceptions to that view.[44] Everything you perceive will have the characteristics opposite of what you discarded. Because you have chosen to see only the ever-changing, what experience have you denied?

The Limitations of Analytic Philosophy

Before we begin I must state the limitations of *analytic philosophy*. From a dualistic point of view, the study of words to define concepts can make comparisons and contrasts tedious. It would be like an ethical and aesthetic

---

[43] *The Way Home p55-57*
[44] This is what selective perception is all about

debate about the difference between pornography and erotic art.

Through the eyes of each individual is an ever-changing cultural context of ever-shifting interpretations. In this place *the perception of uncertainty* reigns. As perceptions become fixed, illusive beliefs become collected as ideologies and thus, hills to die on.[45] Deferring to motivation for the greater good vs. the individual, the *ethicist* might talk about the reasons for the rightness and wrongness of the picture at hand. The *aesthetic* artist would talk about the nature of beauty, which belongs to the eye of each beholder. According to the eye of the beholder, either the pornographic picture is erotic art or the erotic art is pornographic. Or maybe they are neither. No matter how hard you try to deny this in the name of the "absolute," all meaning belongs to the eye of each beholder.

My point is not an argument for either side, it is a demonstration that within each and every context of debate, you believe reality is yours to select! That is why this debate, as well as all other debates, has been endlessly tedious.

The debate does have a resolution that transcends dualistic thinking. However, to get there you have to suspend your ideology.[46] Because meaning does belong to

---

[45] Complexity of form breeds debate while a simple content is its resolution. This principle is true for all debates.

[46] In every society, culturally unique ways of thinking about the world unite people in their behavior. Anthropologists often refer to the body of ideas that people share as ideology. Ideology can be broken down into at least three specific categories: beliefs, values, and ideals. People's beliefs give

the eye of each beholder, the difference between pornography and erotic art is as simple as the words you choose to call it.[47] In Friedrich Nietzsche's world: *All things are subject to interpretation; whichever interpretation prevails at a given time is a function of power and not truth.*

Because perception makes everything uncertain, in denial do you selectively perceive only that which will defend your ideology, to make it appear consistent and thus right. In other words, the way you see anything is to you the right way because that's the way you see it. This is self-deception of circular reasoning at its best. You do believe reality is yours to select while complicating the results of information to make it difficult for you to see its nothingness.

To not take into account mind's propensity to think dualistically, *analytic philosophy's* challenge to clear up problems and confusions concerning issues in the history of philosophy becomes impossible when the bottom line is as always; in the end meaning belongs to the eye of each beholder.

---

them an understanding of how the world works and how they should respond to the actions of others and their environments. People's values tell them the differences between right and wrong or good and bad. Ideals serve as models for what people hope to achieve in life.

[47] No matter how hard you try to hide behind words, the words you choose betray what you believe.

What Are You Looking At?

If the rain comes
They run and hide their heads
They might as well be dead
If the rain comes

When the sun shines
They slip into the shade
And sip their lemonade
When the sun shines

Lennon & McCartney
Rain

One way of looking at the world is based on perception. In the realm of perception, comparisons, degrees, variation, diversity, analysis and evaluations are experienced. This way of looking at the world also provides you with the opportunity to perceive differences of opinion, opposition, conflict, doubt, situation ethics and error in yourself and others. The ideas of magical thinking, superstitions and pseudo-synchronicity[48] belong to this realm.

Magical thinking and superstitions involve sacred texts, rituals of right behaviors and the manipulation of objects for desired outcomes; to appease your god and avoid undesirable outcomes or future punishment. An obvious example of superstition or magical thinking involves beliefs about death. Even though death of a body

---

[48] *Symbols of Power p46-48*

is a natural process of what all bodies do, it is filled with fear, pain, disbelief, loss and ultimate magical conquests that deny what a body does.

Pseudo-synchronicity is the interpretations of coincidences in your life ... situations that seem to make these series of events mean something special to a present event. It is a way to make an ever-changing moment magically special and thus real. For example, "If I hadn't signed up for that class, I never would have met you."

When it comes to interpreting ever-changing events, everything is in a continual state of being up for grabs. So what exactly is it that you are looking at? Does complicating the results of information make it difficult to see its nothingness?

Overcoming Differences

> *I can show you*
> *That when it starts to rain*
> *Everything is the same*
> *I can show you*

Lennon & McCartney
Rain

All of your interpretations of your seemingly multiple life problems involve a comparison of differences or *separation*. Everything that falls apart, decays, disintegrates, is in a constant state of separation. Earth quakes, hurricanes, tornadoes, mud slides are about separation. Anger, killing, the tearing of the flesh is about separation. Sickness of a body in all its forms is about separation. Death is about the idea of separation. The child that is born naked into the world is symbolic of separation and existential abandonment.

Whether it is about the duality of male / female or of a same sex orientation, having sex is about your *attempt* to join through bodies, to undo the separation ... over and over again. The coming together of two bodies to share in a "special love"[49] is the formula for possessiveness, jealousy, conflict and divorce ... unless your love transcends the "special" idea that joining is about bodies. Whether it is about parents, family and friends who seem to come and go, in one form or another all of us play out a perceptual interpretation of separation that is easily misinterpreted as abandonment.

In spite of a pervasive temptation to perceive and interpret people and events as a me – you separateness, we have all experienced *overcoming differences* to remain as friends. Though you may have taken this transcendent experience for granted, many people have risen to the occasion to remain as, or eventually become friends, in spite of the illusive issues that caused a divorce.

In the dream the body's eyes may continue to see differences. But it is the healed mind that does not acknowledge them.[50]

---

[49] That God loves his creation as One does not allow for God's love to be more special for anyone. Therefore, if your love for another is "special" it is not with God's love.
[50] *Symbols of Power p149-151*

When it comes to interpreting the ever-changing through comparison and contrast, your interpretation will be one of separating; the breeding ground for hills to die on. When it comes to joining, seeing commonality, a transcendent experience occurs. So, what exactly is it that you are looking at? Does complicating the results of information make it difficult to see its nothingness?

Non-Duality

Non-duality, *as compared* to the perception of seeing differences, is the other way to look at the world. It is based on the experience of knowing directly, beyond sensation and perception. Because it is the experience beyond any concept of opposition, it cannot be measured or compared. Because it is an experience beyond comparing it cannot be communicated directly through language. It is communicated through the language of analogy, allegory, and metaphor. Non-duality can be studied through the philosophical discipline of *metaphysics.* However, to study it through the eyes of duality is to lose it. That is why thinking in non-dualistic terms are the metaphors that confound dualistic thinking through paradoxes, conundrums and enigmas. For example;

What makes one a master? It is the understanding that they know one thing more than everybody else. They know that they know nothing.

Or; *a renunciate is one who has nothing to renounce. By laying down the position of renunciation, you are free to enjoy times of plenty as well as times of lack.*[51]

Or; *to be free is to recognize your limits.*

Non-dualistic statements defuse the conflict dualistic thinking breeds. They allow your mind room to transcend the battleground of differences. Though non-duality may appear to the rules of empiricism[52] to be a "leap of faith," faith is not needed because non-duality is an experience beyond belief or judgment. It is the experience of looking in a way that brings everything together without comparison or contradiction. Why do you perceive in opposites?

Being and non-being create each other
Difficulty and easy support each other
Long and short define each other
High and low depend on each other
Before and after follow each other

Tao Te Ching #2

According to Carl Jung,[53] it is the principle of your mind to seek integration for peace. By understanding how the

---

[51] *The Way Home p148, p146.* This book is about an exercise in non-dualistic thinking.
[52] Empiricism is the idea that knowledge can only be derived through sense experience
[53] Carl Gustav Jung (1875-1961) was a Swiss psychiatrist who founded the analytical school of psychology. Jung broadened Sigmund Freud's psychoanalytical approach, interpreting mental and emotional disturbances as an attempt to find personal and spiritual wholeness. He later made a distinction between the personal unconscious, the repressed feelings and

personal unconscious integrates with the collective unconscious, Jung theorized that a patient could achieve a state of individuation, or wholeness of self. To overlook the opportunities for inclusion or integration is to seek for the division of differences, which brings your mind into the experience of conflict.

If Jung is accurate, you are seeking both integration and division at the same time. *Projecting the conflict of a divided goal outwards is an attempt to get rid of the conflict within.* This disassociation enables you to believe that there is a world outside of your mind. However, if no thought leaves its source, you always experience what you project. The conflict you see in the world is the *witness* to your denial of the conflict of a mind split within. Jung said "to look out is to dream. To look within is to waken."

If your mind seeks integration and a desire to protect a divided goal, for integrity's sake it will deceive itself into believing that the conflicting goals are the same. And because your mind cannot serve two masters it will have neither. This is why you can have a conflicting view of a loving God who punishes, or why you can grieve and say it's because of love, or why hate is justified in the name of truth, or why you poison the water you drink, or why the fault you see in another you do not see in yourself, or why you can selectively justify killing in instances of "just" wars, or why aborting a baby is wrong but capital punishment is justified, or why aborting a baby is justified

---

thoughts developed during an individual's life, and the collective unconscious, those inherited feelings, thoughts, and memories shared by all humanity.

in the name of "it's my body" but capital punishment is not justified in the name of "two wrongs do not make a right" ... sometimes. This is what the old cliché is all about regarding the left hand not knowing what the right hand is doing. There are no universal ethics in the ever-changing world that can decide what is right and what is wrong. That is why we have all gotten caught up in the mental headaches of dualistic scenarios of being "damned if you do and damned if you don't."

Your power of decision in the world of your perceptive mind is between an ever-changing duality of endless possibilities of nothingness that may as well come down to the grocery line clerk asking you to decide between "paper or plastic."[54] Or, your real power of decision as your one remaining freedom is a choice to transcend the duality of conflict.

Examples of Duality

If wholeness is integration of your mind towards a unified goal, for it to be split or divided of purpose would cause it to be confused or sick. If it is your mind's natural tendency to seek integration towards wholeness, meaning and/or bliss, it is constantly looking for resolution in a place it can't be found, in the world of your divided mind. And, the world of a divided mind would be projected as dualistic in concept described through words like;

---

[54] George Carlin. *The Way Home p55-57*

good & bad (value)
right & wrong (morality)
big & little (size)
strong & weak (power)
hot & cold (degrees)
more & less (amount)
sweet & sour (taste)
loud & soft (sound)
black & white (difference)
pleasure & pain (comfort)
hard & soft (texture)
rested & tired (disposition)
excellence & deficiency (quality)
introverted and extroverted (temperament)
calm and angry (being)
block & flow (resistance)
bright & dim (sight)
permanence & change (paradox)
yesterday & tomorrow (tenses)
free will & determinism (outcome)
 ... to name a few

All concepts are used to compare, measure, frame, and explain, etc., your body's experience of its world through sensation and perception. These comparisons bestow a "value" to the ever-changing that is not intrinsic to it. Its value is assessed *by your mind* according to what it can and cannot do for your body of sensation and perception. You may think these comparisons and distinctions provide for meaning, comfort and survival. But actually, they provide a temporary reprieve from the death of a body. Actually, they are descriptions of a fearful mind's projection of a split mind.[55] Your body does not know intrinsic value. That is a category of a mind led by the dictates of a body to find pleasure and avoid pain.[56] You may think you are "clever, classless and free"[57] but your clever choices for meaning, bliss are limited to all the forms of dualistic thinking that your mind "values" for the comfort and survival of your body. Do you really think that reality is yours to select?

Perception & Uncertainty

Nobody tells it "like it is"
We all tell it "like we see it"

Duality is comparison; it needs a subject and an object to be. Perception is about degrees, levels, comparing the ever-changing against the ever-changing. Because of this, *perception brings the mind into uncertainty.* Because perception brings your mind into uncertainty, there seems to be innumerable ways to look at the world. When you routinely say "I know" you're actually just perceiving degrees of uncertainly.[58]

Knowledge says there is only one way to look at the world. That statement makes no sense when you seem to have innumerable choices between all your perceptions of uncertainty. However, there are two ways of looking at

---

[55] *Symbols of Power p146*
[56] Hedonism is a school of thought that argues that pleasure is the only intrinsic good. In very simple terms, a hedonist strives to maximize pleasure and minimize pain.
[57] John Lennon
[58] *Symbols of Power p34-35*

the world. One way is through all your innumerable choices that the uncertainty of perception brings to you through your mind. The other way is the experience of knowing beyond sensation and perception.

Your continued focus on measuring degrees of ever-changing uncertainty for relevance and meaning is so you can find a security of certainty. However, your search for certainty among evolving data of uncertainty is the reason you continue to collect data of evolving uncertainty. How insane!

There is nothing wrong with the scientific method of collecting data. But does it measure anything of relevance? The scientific method of research assumes a justification for an idea. Then it collects data to generate information. But it collects only the random samples that exist within its assumption ... that the measure of uncertainty can bring meaningful certainty.

Summary

We think in opposites
We talk in opposites
We create in opposites
This is because the mind is in opposition with itself

From a dualistic view of life there are interactions and complications of opposition that fuel all debate. Your mind cannot serve two masters and remain without conflict. Nor can you integrate dualistic thinking with non-dualistic thinking and still have integrity of mind. Your attempt to synthesis, to try to apprehend the eternal and make the temporary meaningful is a violation of your peace of mind. The existentialists argued for integrity by saying "Life is an absurd paradox, a contradiction; a cruel trick that cannot be resolved."[59] You think your experience of dualistic thinking is normal. But it is your experience of how you try to frame chaos as meaningful. This attempt becomes very tiring. There are endless scenarios of "damned if you do and damned if you don't." There is a complication of information that makes it difficult to see its nothingness.

Your experience of opposites is a trick of the mind, a delusion of consciousness, an error of thought projected from the conflict of a split mind. You will not find your bliss in your projection. And a unified mind through dualistic thinking is not possible. To negate dualistic thinking as a way to find peace of mind leaves you with what? Because you cannot choose reality among the uncertainty of perceptive duality your choice will be to transcend dualistic thinking.

Because you use "thinking" to rob you of peace of mind, your need will be to use "thinking" in a way to once again experience "Being" beyond thinking. Practice will be essential ... and your willingness will need to be undivided. One thing you can practice: Whenever you see debate, see duality at work instead. Then you can see the battle of uncertainty for what it is.

---

[59] Heidegger argued that humanity finds itself in an incomprehensible, indifferent world. Human beings can never hope to understand why they are here; instead, each individual must choose a goal and follow it with passionate conviction, aware of the certainty of death and the ultimate meaninglessness of one's life.

Can you hear me?
That when it rains and shines
It's just a state of mind
Can you hear me?

Lennon & McCartney
Rain

C. The Study of Ethics as an Ethical Dilemma

Rules are not made to be broken
They're made to manage chaos
They are broken because
Chaos can't be managed

Introduction

One of the four main branches in philosophy is the study of Ethics. The word *ethics* is translated from the Greek as principles or standards of human conduct. It is sometimes called morals from the Latin "mores" or customs. The study of ethics has to do with social order, stability; the glue that some presume holds society together. More specifically, the study of ethics involves the question of motivation for ethical or moral behaviors and attitudes.

A Brief History

The Sophist[60] Protagoras[61] taught that human judgment is subjective and that one's perception is valid

---

[60] Sophia, the Greek word for "wisdom" is a central idea in Hellenistic philosophy and religion, Platonism, Gnosticism, Orthodox Christianity, Esoteric Christianity, as well as Christian mysticism. The word Sophists was originally applied by the ancient Greeks to learned men, most of whom concluded that truth and morality were essentially matters of opinion.

[61] Protagoras (480?-411? BC) was a Greek philosopher who

only for oneself. The Sophist Gorgias[62] argued that nothing exists; that if anything does exist, human beings could not know it; and that if they did know it, they could not communicate that knowledge. Other Sophists, such as Thrasymachus, believed that might makes right.

Socrates opposed the Sophists, as represented in the dialogues of his pupil Plato.[63] Virtue is knowledge; people will be virtuous if they know what virtue is; and vice, or evil, is the result of ignorance. Thus, according to Socrates, education can make people moral.

Since the ancient Greeks, this has all been debated ... again and again. Is there anything new under the sun?

The Concept of Natural Law

Through the middle ages the church was exemplified as the supreme authority for God. Coming out of the Middle Ages was "The Age of Enlightenment;"[64] a term

---

was the first thinker to call himself a Sophist. The basis of his speculation was the doctrine that nothing is absolutely good or bad, true or false, and that each individual is therefore his or her own final authority; this belief is summed up in his saying: "Man is the measure of all things."

[62] Gorgias (circa 485-380 BC) was a Greek Sophistic philosopher whose philosophy is viewed as nihilistic.

[63] Plato (428?-347 BC) was a Greek philosopher who is considered one of the most creative and influential thinkers in Western philosophy. Plato expressed the idea that by its very nature anything involving perception and change would be imperfect. He was Socrates student and Aristotle's teacher.

[64] The precursors of the Enlightenment can be traced to the 17th century and earlier. They include the philosophical rationalists René Descartes and Baruch Spinoza, the political philosophers Thomas Hobbes and John Locke.

used to describe the trends in thought and letters in Europe and the American colonies during the 18th century prior to the French Revolution. The phrase was frequently employed by writers of the period itself, convinced that they were emerging from centuries of darkness and ignorance into a new age enlightened by reason, science, and a respect for humanity. "Reason" seen as the primary cause for humanity's evolution was to be the new God. But what does "reason" mean? To Isaac Newton[65] it was clear that gravity was the cause of motion. To John Locke[66] it was clear that the motion of the political universe was caused by scarcity. To the Deists,[67] God was the first cause.

---

[65] Sir Isaac Newton (1642-1727) was an English physicist, mathematician, and natural philosopher, considered one of the most important scientists of all time.

[66] John Locke (1632-1704) was an English philosopher who founded the school of empiricism. Locke's empiricism emphasizes the importance of the experience of the senses in pursuit of knowledge rather than intuitive speculation or deduction. Knowledge, to Locke is not innate, but comes only from experience and observation guided by reason.

[67] Deism was a rationalist religious philosophy that flourished in the 17th and 18th centuries, particularly in England. Generally, Deists held that a certain kind of religious knowledge (sometimes called natural religion) is either inherent in each person or accessible through the exercise of reason, but they denied the validity of religious claims based on revelation or on the specific teachings of any church. Their emphasis on reason and their opposition to fanaticism and intolerance greatly influenced John Locke, David Hume and in France, the writer, philosopher Voltaire (1694-1778) who was one of the leaders of the Enlightenment.

David Hume[68] asked; "what are we talking about when we talk about something we can't see or feel as first cause? That God is to be construed as a first cause is as much an assumption as a committee of gods being a first cause."[69] Not only does Hume's skepticism ask whether or not people are jumping to the wrong conclusion about a primary cause, but to those who followed in his school of thought, the question was; why do people so universally jump to such a conclusion?

Natural Law in ethical philosophy, theology, law, and social theory are principles *assumed* to be permanent characteristics of human nature that can serve as standards for evaluating conduct and civil laws.[70] "We

---

[68] David Hume (1711-1776) was a Scottish historian and philosopher, who influenced the development of skepticism and empiricism, two schools of philosophy. Hume endeavored to prove that reason and rational judgments are merely habitual associations of distinct sensations or experiences. Hume held that the concept of right and wrong is not rational but arises from a regard for one's own happiness. The supreme moral good, according to his view, is benevolence, an unselfish regard for the general welfare of society that Hume regarded as consistent with individual happiness. *Treatise of Human Nature* (3 volumes) embodies the essence of his thinking. It is a perplexing read.

[69] "Committee of gods" referring to the Greek pantheon or temple of gods.

[70] Stoicism as a school of philosophy, founded in ancient Greece is the principle that good lies not in external objects, but in the state of the soul itself. All people are manifestations of the one universal spirit and should, according to the Stoics, live in brotherly love and readily help one another. They held that external differences such as rank and wealth are of no

hold these truths to be self-evident that all men are created equal," is a statement of natural law. The statement is not an answer to the questions of Hume's skepticism over first cause; it merely pushes through the skepticism. Nor do you get caught up into quibbling over whose first cause is the right one. The founders of the American Republic assumed there to be an inherent common sense that moved them to a higher moral ground. This inherent common sense was the justification for a revolution over their oppressors.

All men are created equal, right? Does that include women? Most women are not as strong as most men. Does that make them less equal than men? Some men of color are not as equal as other men of other colors. Does majority and minority status have something to do with deciding what equality is; or is it money, or appearances, or education, or a combination of these within a changing cultural, social context? Some bodies are frailer than others. What's equal about that? Some people have physical challenges that others don't. What's equal about that? Some people are smarter than others. Others are mentally handicapped. What's equal about that? Some women have a greater appearance of beauty. Some do not. That's not fair! And does that mean men can't be called beautiful? Some people exhibit enormous courage under pressure. Others run like cowards. What's equal about that? Some people seem to have common sense about life decisions. What should we do with the stupid

---

importance in social relationships. Before the rise of Christianity, Stoics recognized and advocated the brotherhood of humanity and the natural equality of all human beings.

ones? And what's equal about being stupid? And what is stupid? How do we define it? And where is the book on political correctness on how to nicely call someone stupid without violating your freedom of speech? Is there an understanding of right and wrong inherent within each of us? And if so, what is "self-evident" through the world of an ephemeral[71] body?

Although the fathers of the American Republic stood upon the principle, "We hold these truths to be self-evident that all men are created equal," they could not transcend the issue of slavery. They had to set it aside for another generation to figure out so they could form "a more perfect union."

Through the mind frame of a body/self-idea no two things are alike. In fact, nothing is as it seems. Ever-changing physical differences, behavioral inconsistencies, comparisons of mental aptitude, make judgment arbitrary. No two minds embraced in physical bodies will interpret anything exactly the same. *We hold this truth to be self-evident, that those who embrace the mind frame of a body/self-idea will experience violation.*

"We hold these truths to be self-evident that all men are created equal," means what in the light of the ever-changing? Is reality yours to select? What does the data suggest?

---

[71] Ever-changing

Ethical Approaches to Life Situations

Throw away holiness and wisdom and people will be a hundred times happier
Throw away morality and justice and people will do the right thing
Throw away industry and profit and there won't be thieves
If these three aren't enough
Just stay in your center of the circle and let all things take their course

Tao Te Ching #19

Adherents to **Moral Absolutism** may base their point of view on a humanistic[72] law such as "Thou shall not kill." And though killing is wrong, some say there are certain justifiable, noble, patriotic, "moral" reasons to kill. The life of an individual body is *absolutely* sacred ... oh umm ... except in some situations, like self-defense, capital punishment or abortion. But then again the life of a fetus is not really a life; or is it?

How does one decide what situations are to be the exceptions? And can those exceptions be counted on to be always absolute? The Geneva Convention does not have rules on how to kill people. But it does have rules on how you should not kill people. How confusing.

Historically, **Religious Absolutism** assumed preordained rights of the few to rule. That was the

---

[72] Humanism in philosophy emphasizes the dignity and worth of the individual. A basic premise of humanism is that people are rational beings who possess within themselves the capacity for truth and goodness.

political justification that monarchy was based on, especially in France and England. Religious absolutism tries magically to make the ever-changing eternal by justifying its existence through sacred writings and historical fictions of its founders. For example it is written in the Bible; "You shall not lie with a male as one lies with a female; it is an abomination."[73] And in the same book, "you may acquire male and female slaves from the pagan nations that are around you."[74] To defend a belief as absolute by taking the cultural context out of the text not only betrays the lack of an honest approach to understanding the text but also, it demeans the text as a whole as being irrelevant. Also, "the Law written in their hearts, their conscience bearing witness"[75] is problematic. There are so many different rules that justify "righteous conduct" that God must have written different absolutes on each of our hearts. Religious fanaticism and holy wars are all about "With God on Our Side."

Religious absolutism cannot escape the exceptions that an ever-changing culture supplies except through the self-delusion of magical thinking; the seeds of terrorism.

Regarding a **Pantheistic View,**[76] Spinoza, not unlike tribal cultures, expressed a philosophy that identified God with nature. Without the magical thinking of rituals, Spinoza asserted that all things are morally neutral from the point of view of eternity; only human needs and

---

[73] Leviticus 18:22

[74] Leviticus 25:44. These texts have been used to defend and condemn lifestyles.

[75] Romans 2:15

[76] Pantheism is the doctrine that identifies the universe (Greek pan, "all") with God (Greek theos).

interests determine what is considered good and evil, or right and wrong.

For the lover of the outdoors, it is a tempting view for the understanding of how life works in the ever-changing.

Utilitarianism[77] is the doctrine that says what is helpful is good. In other words, the ethical value of conduct is determined by the usefulness of its results. The term utilitarianism is more specifically applied to the proposition that the supreme objective of moral action is the achievement of the greatest happiness for the greatest number. The utilitarian theory of ethics is generally opposed to ethical doctrines of an inner sense or conscience of right and wrong dependent on the will of God. The new god is the Utilitarian collective hunch called society. Economics, politics, law and sociology become society's most ardent disciples. "The end justifies the means" becomes society's due process. However, who will decide what the greatest happiness for the greatest number is to be? Adolph Hitler? Mahatma Gandhi? Joseph Stalin? Mother Theresa?

Social Pragmatists such as William James[78] do not believe that a single absolute idea of goodness or justice exists, but rather that these concepts are changeable and depend on the context in which they are being discussed. James was opposed to absolute metaphysical systems and argued against doctrines that describe reality as a unified,

---

[77] Jeremy Bentham (1748-1832) was a British philosopher, economist, and jurist, who founded the doctrine of utilitarianism.

[78] William James (1842-1910) was an American philosopher and psychologist who was one of the developers of the philosophy of pragmatism.

monolithic whole. "In those days ... every man did what was right in his own eyes."[79] In the light of everything always changing, this approach makes contextual sense.

Immanuel Kant's[80] *Categorical Imperative* expressed that no matter how intelligently one acts, the *results* of human actions are subject to accident and circumstance. Therefore, the morality of an act must not be judged by its consequence, but only by its motivation. In other words, it is your effort that counts, not the outcome.

Doesn't life teach that even with the best of intentions, things can go awry? Yet, you are told that "Under no condition is ignorance of the law a justification for the breaking of that law," ... unless you can argue the insanity plea successfully.

The Existential Twist of Fate Gone Awry

Kierkegaard devoted much of his philosophical writing to his own struggles with faith. Against the current background of an impersonal Hegelian philosophy of choices, in his book *Fear and Trembling*[81] Kierkegaard

---

[79] Judges 21:25

[80] Immanuel Kant (1724-1804) was a German philosopher who is considered by many the most influential thinker of modern times. Kant aimed to resolve disputes between empirical and rationalist approaches. The former asserted that all knowledge comes through experience; the latter maintained that reason and innate ideas were prior. Kant argued that experience is purely subjective without first being processed by pure reason. He also said that using reason without applying it to experience only leads to theoretical illusions.

[81] The title is a reference to a line from Philippians 2:12, where Paul encourages the congregation to "... work out your

introduces his concept of *The Teleological Suspension of the Ethical.* Often associated with Christian and religious philosophy, teleology is the belief in and study of "final causes" in nature. Thus, in Kierkegaard's case, the teleological suspension of the ethical refers to an abandonment of normal religious beliefs in favor of the "final cause" or "ultimate cause" of God's will. In this teleological suspension of the ethical, normal moral and ethical dictates are transcended in favor of an absolute and unquestioning faith in God.

Kierkegaard's example of this involves the biblical characters of Abraham and Isaac. God commanded Abraham to sacrifice Isaac, a dictate that obviously is in stark contrast to moral norms about murder and parental love and protection. However, Kierkegaard believes that there is a higher authority than ethical norms and that Abraham was answering to this higher authority in God. Thus Abraham committed a teleological suspension of the ethical and did the right thing in being willing to sacrifice Isaac in order to please God.

It is important to note that Kierkegaard does not condone performing immoral actions and claiming they were in the name of God. He argues that a person must first recognize, understand, and embrace social norms and normal ethical dictates in order to reach a moral level where they are able to follow a higher power in the form of God. Being able to engage in a teleological suspension of the ethical is the highest level of moral development for Kierkegaard and therefore Abraham is an admirable

salvation with fear and trembling."

character, even though what he did with Isaac may seem troubling at first glance.

Through the perception of uncertainty, Kierkegaard's teleological suspension of the ethical can easily be misused as "the end justifies the means." The suspension of the ethical for an "ultimate cause" means different things to different people. Justifying killing in "The name of God" is one of the many zealous abuses committed throughout the history of human kind. Terrorism is justified through the idea that "my moral view is more right or absolute over yours." Also, there were people who lied, bribed, forged documents and even killed to protect the Jews and others from the Nazis. Were they justified in doing those things? Is there a higher purpose through love that transcends conventional ethical norms?

One of Nietzsche's fundamental contentions was that traditional values (represented primarily by Christianity) had lost their power in the lives of individuals. Nietzsche maintained that all human behavior is motivated by the will to power. In its positive sense, the will to power is not simply power over others, but the power over oneself that is necessary for creativity. According to Nietzsche, the masses (whom he termed the herd or mob) conform to tradition, whereas his ideal "Übermensch," overman/superman is secure, independent, and highly individualistic. Though I do not believe Nietzsche meant his philosophy to play this way, the Nazis used the concept of "Das Übermensch" to justify their totalitarian[82] philosophy.

---

[82] Totalitarianism in political science, system of government and ideology is where all social, political, economic,

Jean-Paul Sartre's[83] psychology asserted that all individuals cannot escape their own decisions and that the recognition of one's absolute freedom of choice is the necessary condition for authentic human existence. In his later philosophic work Sartre argued that the influence of modern society over the individual is so great as to produce "serialization" or a loss of self. Moving towards a Marxist[84] determinism Sartre argued that individual power and freedom can only be regained through group revolutionary action.

You say you want a revolution
Well you know we all want to change the world
You tell me that it's evolution
Well you know we all want to change the world
But when you talk about destruction
*Don't you know that you can count me **out ... in***

Lennon & McCartney
Revolution 1

Ethically speaking, "violence" can be justified. You just have to call it another name.

---

intellectual, cultural, and spiritual activities are subordinated to the purposes of the rulers of a state.
[83] Jean-Paul Sartre (1905-1980) was a French philosopher, dramatist, novelist, and political journalist, and a leading exponent of existentialism.
[84] Karl Marx (1818-1883) was a German political philosopher and revolutionist, cofounder with Friedrich Engels of scientific socialism (modern communism), and is considered as one of the most influential thinkers of modern times.

Sexual Preference / Orientation[85]

*Because morality involves the self as a body, your
investment in the body draws you into issues of morality*

If Heraclitus[86] is right, that all things are in a state of
continuous flux and therefore stability is an illusion, to
identify with a body as "you" would be to invest in
something that is illusively unstable. If you are more than
just a body, to view "you" as a body would be identity
confusion. And attempting to identify with the temporary
demonstrates your involvement in the denial of trying to
accomplish an impossible task.[87] Only confusion and
frustration about everything you perceive can follow.
Ethics/morality become facades, rules for conduct used
to try and organize, make meaningful an ever-changing
that can never have meaning. Society becomes a
collective hunch fraught with exceptions and
contradictions.

Psychologically speaking, someone having an identity
crisis or confusion of identity, has traditionally been
explained as those who "prefer" deviant sexual behaviors.
The argument that tries to understand ones deviation
from the norm as identity confusion caused by traumatic
childhood experiences (nurture) faces to many
exceptions. However, *a trauma before your so-called*

[85] I fully realize that the choice of words here is a battle ground.
[86] Heraclitus (540?-480? BC) was a Greek philosopher who
maintained that all things are in a state of continuous flux, that
stability is an illusion.
[87] This is what a frustrated learner is all about. *Symbols of
Power p98*

conception as to the cause for your confusion about identifying as a body/self-identity is universally conceivable. And this conceivability includes everybody ... while you busily look out upon your mind's world focusing on peculiar little details of data that tempt you to conclude how different you are from others ... keeping you distracted from the deeper issue like ... why do you have confusion about everything you perceive and are not aware of this confusion?

Genetics

Genetics may carry a blueprint of inclinations or mannerisms (nature), but you are always free to choose how you perceive the *so-called* limitations of a body. Science may eventually isolate a gene that seems to explain a sexual deviation from the norm, but in the ever-changing flux, it will be fraught with illusive exceptions.

As with all issues, genetic engineering involves a "self," the controversy of our offspring. Shouldn't it be good to engineer humans that are resistant to disease or are less vulnerable to heart disease? Or is this tampering with nature, playing God? And just like the splitting of an atom for energy or the development of opium for a derivative called morphine for pain, are they not also used as avenues for large-scale killing and addiction?

These examples of contradiction are but tips of the iceberg that attest to a bigger picture than the duality of thinking that nature vs. nurture presents.[88] Why are there contradictory exceptions about everything you perceive?

---

[88] *Symbols of Power p119-127*

There is a complexity of data (form) that does not imply a complexity of content. Data can be better understood as generalized under the umbrella of a principled content.

What You Think

Even though you experience what you think
What you think is not what you are

Your mind is not part of the body's process of natural selection, procreation, and survival. You have unknowingly decided to limit your creative expression through the vessel you call a body. You are emotionally invested and stifled by something you are not. The wedding of thought and form brings alive the controversy of nature vs. nurture. Though this controversy is irrelevant to the transcendent mind, how you live and clash with one another within your self-prescribed limitations is the subject of ethics.

Whether it is God, nation, or right living,[89] what you value as a bottom line does not make it absolute as much as it makes it your hill to die on.

You have given up your reality of mind to the insanity of a body fraught with contradictions, exceptions, limitations and violations. Your bliss is not to be found there. Your challenge is to think out of the box!

---

[89] Whatever that is?

Summary

The more prohibitions you have
The less virtuous people will be

Tao Te Ching #57

When it comes to the study of ethics regarding its motivation for attitudes and behaviors, there is no end to the conundrum. The philosophical possibilities, discussions, debates have always been as endless as the stars. There are ethical debates about sex, sexual orientation/preference, what constitutes a family, partnership, capital punishment, abortion, politics, economics, technology, professional conduct, culture, ethnicity, prejudice, to name only a few. When it comes to the idea of consensus, history demonstrates that it is sometimes a pleasant fantasy and sometimes a totalitarian terror, always fleeting.[90] Majority consensus does not make right. What is considered a consensus? Is there not a consensus among the minority totalitarian elite? If all standards of conduct depend upon a context and culture that is ever-changing, all standards of conduct are illusive. Social consensus is an ever-changing collective hunch.

Rules are but an attempt to make chaos look like order

---

[90] "Might makes right" is a cute cliché when you are the mighty righteous one who gets to write the history.

Apparently, morality belongs to the eye of the beholder, sanctioned through a collective hunch as to what society at large believes, always subject to exceptions given the context of the moment and argued about as to what motivates it and what should be punishable. What is morality in the light of this? Is it the conventional lie that things are done for ethical reasons? Is it the ethical truth that things are done for the sake of convention?

> *For there is nothing good or bad*
> *But thinking makes it so*

William Shakespeare
Hamlet; Act 2, Scene 2

Is there 1) a violation one is incarnated with, 2) projected through unconscious guilt as a world, 3) played out as a socially conditioned ideology, 4) needing to be managed through rules of conduct we call ethics and 5) denied as being played out as demonstrated through your resistance to seeing the obvious?

The world you seem to be born into out of a violation is well hidden from your view. And even though 350 years ago the Age of Enlightened Reason espoused practical facts to abolish magical thinking, fanatical superstition continues to play over and over again through cleverly contrived forms; and not just in developing countries who seem to be behind the evolutionary curve.

Ever-changing background (the stage) seems to indicate an evolution of progress. Yet, the same issues of ethics and morality are played out over and over again.

Either an ever-changing educational curriculum has failed to raise us above or change a flawed social conditioning, or it is all irrelevant. Or it is a matter of waking up individually from a re-occurring dream of guilt.

There is a battle being waged in your mind, projected as a world of conflict and then covered up with rules for order, so you can't see where the source of the conflict comes from. Is there a gripping fear underneath it all that won't allow you release? Would you rather avoid these questions because they uncover a discomfort around the idea that there is no such thing as stability in the ever-changing? Is there an unconscious guilt[91] that explains your resistance to and therefore denial of the obvious?

You transcend the duality of a split mind by being open not to just a change of behavior or modified beliefs but rather by being a mind open to receive correction on a fundamental level. The study of ethics demonstrates that the ever-changing is not a place to find meaning. What is definitive here? Is reality yours to select? What does the data suggest?

---

[91] Sigmund Freud (1856-1939) was an Austrian physician, neurologist, and founder of psychoanalysis. In his clinical observations Freud found evidence for the mental mechanisms of repression and resistance. He described repression as a device operating unconsciously to make the memory of painful or threatening events inaccessible to the conscious mind. Resistance is defined as the unconscious defense against awareness of repressed experiences in order to avoid the resulting anxiety or punishment.

D. The Drama of Child Development Theories[92]

Show me an earth, where the birth of a child, disguised as the Word, can be recognized

James Seals
Earth

A Brief History

The importance of childhood as a unique period of development became a topic of conversation in the 17th and 18th centuries, as reflected in the writings of two important European thinkers.

The English philosopher John Locke argued that the newborn infant comes into the world with no inherited predispositions, but rather with a mind as a tabula rasa (Latin for "blank slate") that is gradually filled with ideas, concepts, and knowledge from experiences in the world. He concluded that the quality of early experiences, particularly how children are raised and educated, shapes the direction of a child's life. Later, the French philosopher Jean Jacques Rousseau[93] claimed that

---

[92] Calling them "theories" is enough to question the study of child development as being anything but reasonable, predictable, conclusive or explainable.

[93] Jean Jacques Rousseau (1712-1778) was a French philosopher, social and political theorist, musician, botanist, and one of the most eloquent writers of the Age of Enlightenment.

children at birth are innately good, not evil, and that their natural tendencies should be protected against the corrupting influences of society.

A Brief Overview of Contemporary Theories

There are four main theories of child development: psychoanalytic,[94] learning,[95] cognitive,[96] and socio-cultural.[97] Each offers ideas into the forces guiding childhood growth. *Each also has limitations,* which is why many developmental scientists use more than one theory to guide their thinking about the growth of children.

Many developmental scientists believe that later experiences *can modify* or even reverse early influences; studies show that even when early experiences are

---

[94] According to Freud, early experiences shape one's personality for an entire lifetime, and that psychological problems in adulthood *may have* their origins in difficult or traumatic childhood experiences.

[95] John B Watson (1878-1958) was an American psychologist, founder and leading exponent of the school of psychology known as behaviorism, which restricts psychology to the study of objectively observable behavior and explains behavior in terms of stimulus and response.

[96] Jean Piaget (1896-1980) was a Swiss psychologist, best known for his pioneering work on the development of intelligence in children. Noam Chomsky (1928-) is an American linguist, educator, and political activist.

[97] Lev Semionovich Vygotsky (1896–1934) was a Soviet psychologist, whose work on language and linguistic development is based on his supposition that higher cognitive processes are a product of social development; that children's interaction with adults contributes to the development of skills.

traumatic or abusive, considerable recovery occurs. From this point of view it can be said that early experiences *may influence*, but do not necessarily determine later characteristics. It is important to note that *so-called* traumatic experiences have been seen as opportunities for growth rather than obstacles. Overused clichés such as "What doesn't kill you can cure you" and "Your greatest opportunities come through your greatest challenges" demonstrate this.

Why do some children perceive events as traumatizing while others do not? Why do some adults try to teach children that what was traumatic to them should also be traumatic to a child? Then there are children who go through therapy, supposedly dealing with denial because they did not interpret their life event as traumatic. Their task becomes the undoing of an adult drama trauma that was taught they should have but never was. Where are the *outcome studies* of children considered by others to have early traumatic or disadvantaged socio-economic experiences, who themselves do not perceive those experiences that way?

Theories of why we are the way we are, remain inconclusive while the uncertainty of perception does make the observer a personally biased participant.

Socialized out of Fear

Sigmund Freud believed we were socialized out of fear.[98] If you think about it, wasn't fear a big part of growing up? If you were not able to adapt or be socialized by denying your dilemma of a world that could never make sense, the

---

[98]Oedipus complex for boys and the Electra complex for girls

feeling of incompletion would be overwhelming.[99] And so it is, to look for a place to fit in the world you must constantly search outside rather than reflect. Your quest to survive in the world is a constant avoidance of fear from birth to death.

When they tortured and scared you for twenty odd years
Then they expect you to pick a career
When you can't really function you're so full of fear

John Lennon
Working Class Hero

Freud found evidence for the mental mechanisms of unconscious repression defended from awareness by unconscious resistance. Erroneously, these mechanisms have been attributed to childhood compensations in their upbringing. However, regardless of upbringing, these mechanisms are attributes of all of us. Did you bring these mental mechanisms with you? Are you repressing a decision made from the other side of the veil that caused you to be born? Are you playing out this forgotten psychic trauma/drama, projected as a distortion untrue and believing it to be a result of social conditioning?

If there already is a "you" before you were born, your denial of this fact would be the breeding ground for all fear. And in your first experience of this illusion of change (to try to be what you are not), you would experience the fear of abandonment. That is why change is always fearful, needing to be resisted. You have to admit that you

---

[99] The motivating basis for suicide is a spiritual dilemma with no exit but death in view.

Symbols of Power in Philosophy

do have resistance to change with all kinds of reasons why. The most obviously vague reason is because "I am uncomfortable with change."

If you are not what you think you are, you will experience fear. To get rid of the fear, you will project it and as Freud believed, disassociate yourself from your awareness of this projection (denial). If the image you project is fearful, it will be projected as unknown to you. You can't know your projection if you don't know you. In the absence of knowing you, for security sake, and through the process of physical development and mental socialization, you will try to make your projection meaningfully real. Because your goal is to attempt the impossible -- make meaning out of a fearful projection of what you are not, you will experience frustration and ongoing fear. To not know is replaced by doubt, belief, faith, hope, magical thinking and fear.

In the light of who you really are, all these associations of so-called development become meaningless. You were not socialized out of fear. You brought it with you. Complicating the results of information does make it difficult to see its nothingness. What does the data suggest?

Perceptual Temper Tantrum

Children that seem to misbehave are easily labeled as oppositional defiant. If you look closer it seems to be an impulsive reaction to their environment. If you look even closer, it is actually an impulsive reaction to their projection. A perceptual temper tantrum is just that, a reaction to your distortion of what you think you need or how things should be ... right now! Simply stated, some children struggle more with adapting to their own projection of a world not real. Children remind you all the time that their reactions to their outer world are their reflection of their inner world.

Perceptions become stable when beliefs become fixed. Until then, adolescence for some is a roller coaster ride of drama and despair projected from within. Adolescents remind you all the time that their reactions to their outer world are a reflection of their inner world.

Though you may be into feelings, your own socialization has been an intense intellectual experience, focused on understanding your world through the body you assume to be. Because your mind naturally gravitates towards abstraction, this intellectually concrete, discrete and goal orientated focus to be socialized, takes work to master. It takes work to deny what you naturally know.

Hypocrisy runs rampant among all of us because the myth of living a perfect life in terms of behavior is a self-defeating goal[100] that will drive you insane. As long as you are confused about what you are, you will play your and others behaviors out as temptations to judge success and failure. This deception will hide your real dilemma.

Just like children who seem to misbehave, your mental adaptation to an unnatural experience of trying to fit in as labeled through physical stages of development is about trying to make your projection work. Learning may be change, but trying to master an impossible lesson makes for a frustrated student.

---

[100] *The Way Home p27*

A Socially Conditioned View

Social conditioning skews how you perceive certain life events. There is a socially conditioned *view* that selectively assumes someone should be traumatized by a certain event and if they are not they are in denial.[101] There is also a socially conditioned view that only selects those cases that *seem* to have a cause and effect correlation of "trauma" and "dysfunction" to prove a point.

In the past, many were taught to believe their unresolved present issue had something to do with a blocked memory of a traumatic past event. Also, though the exceptions were massive and largely ignored, there was a time that it was believed that children were problematic because they did not bond early on with their mother. You can always *select* an example to prove your point. However, the point is that social conditioning is not a relevant cause because the contradictions are colossal. There is a socially conditioned view that does not see that its *view* of child development is a socially conditioned view when the bigger picture of exceptions clearly demonstrates that it is not. In other words, you defend social conditioning as a cause for how your children turn out when you have been socially conditioned to selectively see life that way.

It is often stated, actually overstated, as to how environment impacts child development. For example, it is usually asked "What is it in this adolescent's environment that caused him to want to go into a school

---

[101] Transference is about trying to make your unresolved misperceptions as an issue about or for someone else.

and kill his fellow students?" Media promotes dramatized speculation that avoids looking at a deeper dilemma. It is also commonly stated that with all the changes and pressures our kids face these days, it becomes understandable as to why some of them have problems that they act out through their environment. Although nihilism[102] may be an accurate explanation for what the world is all about, the dilemma of child/adolescent development is not a matter of ever-changing environment. Ever-changing environment has been just that from the beginning ... ever-changing! Because complexity of ever-changing form does not imply complexity of content, the dilemma of our children has been the same from the beginning of time.

Your hidden belief that you are alienated from Source is a powerfully illusive distraction played out in innumerable forms, social conditioning being one of them

What looks like social conditioning is merely the form in which your alienation is being acted out, through the customs and culture that time and history present.

Though none of us do it perfectly, most of us can work within a social contract. Actually, because of the uncertainty of perception within the ever-changing, no one does anything perfectly. Why are these days so different from the days of the Greeks or Romans or the Middle Ages or even our modern times of the passing 20th century?[103] All ages have experienced the pressures

---

[102] Nihilism is a viewpoint that traditional values and beliefs are unfounded and that existence is senseless and useless.

of feast and famine, disease and health, war and peace, developmental tasks into tribal belonging. We have all grown up in an environment of social pressure and fear. The only thing different and yet always the same is that the so-called evolving forms of ever-changing nothingness is ever-changing. Among 19th century philosophers, Arthur Schopenhauer[104] was among the first to contend that at its core, the universe is not a rational place; that the ever-changing is not evolving.

Evolution is an illusion of conditioned thinking
To see progress in the ever-changing spin is self-deception

Your spiritual dilemma of alienation has always been the same. The way it is played out depends on the social/cultural forms of that particular time. It is tempting to explain present issues as something uniquely different than times past. It is the belief that complex ever-changing forms have a complex and different content.

---

[103] *Symbols of Power p83-85*
[104] Arthur Schopenhauer (1788–1860) was a German philosopher best known for his book *The World as Will and Representation* in which he claimed that our world is driven by a continually dissatisfied will, continually seeking satisfaction. Influenced by Eastern philosophy, he maintained that the "truth was recognized by the sages of India." Consequently, his solutions to suffering were similar to those of Vedantic and Buddhist thinkers (e.g., asceticism). His faith in "transcendental ideality" rather than an evolving awareness led him to accept atheism.

Bullying has always been and will always be. Fist fights in school seemingly has progressed to knife fights, to street or gang fights, to shootings in schools. The basic dilemma of alienation always looks different as it plays out throughout our ever-changing history of custom and culture. The way alienation plays out depends on the cultural context of that time.

Social conditioning does occur. Environmental factors of influence can weigh in as adjustments in a child's development. But these are merely the effects of a self in alienation with itself rather than a cause of social alienation. Complexity of form does not imply complexity of content. Don't confuse social conditioning as being a cause with meaningful correlations of effect. It has none. The world is not a rational place to find meaning.

Criteria & Performance

As your body changes throughout its body life span you are evaluated according to particular life span developmental tasks.

Simply stated, at birth you are given a name and a series of numbers[105] (for further identification) to keep for the rest of your body life. You are also evaluated according to sex type, physical appearance and motor skills, to name a few. In school you are measured by letters (grades) that represent levels of curricular accomplishment. Grading on a curve is the measured response of your performance against the performance of others. Self-appeal is also measured by academic achievement, sex appeal, popularity, sports, and

---

[105] Social Security numbers

extracurricular activities. The value these measures have *solely depends on* your investment in peer influence and future possibilities.

Out of pressure to conform, you take on values you did not choose. "Who you are and what you do" they tell you "is the same thing." But sometimes, they tell you "it is two different things."

> *They hate you if you're clever*
> *And they despise a fool*
> *Till you're so fucking crazy*
> *You can't follow their rules*

> John Lennon
> Working Class Hero

Attempting to live an unachievable contradiction between what you are and what you should be, you bury the contradiction by not thinking about it.[106] You spend your time trying to live according to vague guidelines that have been passed down to you. Your main value will be to produce, consume and pay taxes. In this way you become a productive member of society. Now you have value. At times, on a personal level, you may even find some kind of vague ever-fleeting fulfillment.

Job evaluations selectively reflect your performance strengths and weaknesses. They also justify reward through pay. This makes for a happier and more productive member of society, right? With all this busy

---

[106] Cognitive dissonance is when a person's beliefs and actions are not logically consistent with one another. To live a lie you have to believe the lie is true.

activity to produce excellence, does anyone ask, "what is it all for? What is excellence in the ever-changing?"

> *If this is success*
> *Then something's awfully wrong*
> *Cause I bought the dream*
> *And I had to play along*

> Van Morrison
> Not Feeling It Anymore

No matter how hard you try not to think about your existential contradiction, living a mediocre life of conformity cannot avoid the stress of personal alienation. Stress is the result of fearing you will not measure up to the task you identify with as your reflection of success or failure. While, what you are to measure up to, you are not always sure of. You fear a vague punishment of failing at something that may or may not be yours to accomplish. You may even entreat others to take up the mantel with you. "It's your right, your responsibility and your moral duty to be true" you spout. "True to what?" you may question quietly while scratching your head. As long as you keep the accomplishment concrete you can have some measure of success while fearing the possibility of failure. It takes enormous courage, insanity or transcendence to think out of the traditional box of assumed norms.

What are criteria?
Standards of measure that categorize behavioral responsiveness
What are categorized responses?
Assumptions about the "norm" based on the parameters of criteria
What is the norm?
Degrees of deviations on the bell shaped curve
What does all this mean?
Whatever you want it to mean

Complicating the results of information does make it difficult to see its nothingness.

Your Search for Validation

To measure or compare is to look outside. To look outside is to look for value in something that will demonstrate your worth. If you believe that what happens outside measures your worth, then to look for worth outside is a demonstration of you not knowing what you are on the inside. So what you find is many comparisons of possibilities ... and always fleeting doubt. But you will never find what you are looking for because what you are looking for cannot be found outside. And you will never measure up because how do you measure up to a "you" you do not know against the ever-changing you are not? To measure up becomes an impossible and therefore frustrating task of successive successes and failures according to how you interpret what is accomplishment in your life events. Yet, you need to strive until you find this out. Why are you so tired?

Because a futile undertaking to nowhere takes immense effort.

What you are trying to measure up to
Is as changeable as the ocean tides
Is as nebulous as the stars in the sky
Is as selective as each individual point of view
What are you trying to measure up to?

Given the data, how do you explain your continued denial of the obvious?

Mind over Matter

Whatever you identify with you adapt to
But that does not change what you already are

If you are projecting a body image, there is a "you" that remembers the other side. Nicolai Hartmann[107] reacting against the neo-Kantian view that the mind *constructs reality* through the inherent forms of thought argued that *reality is prior to thought.* In other words, when parents are momentarily free from a conditioned or constructed[108] perspective, they readily admit that there was something about each child that was "a done deal" when that child was born.[109] The temptation is to assume influences throughout a child's development as causes of why

---

[107] Nicolai Hartmann (1882-1950) was a German idealist philosopher and one of the central figures in early 20th-century German thought.
[108] fabricated
[109] *Symbols of Power p120-124*

people end up the way they do rather than view those mislabeled causes as effects of a larger condition, a greater dilemma, a bigger paradigm. For example, there is no conclusive reason as to why a child is a bully or why a child is bullied. Again, there are *always* too many exceptions to draw a conclusion of cause and effect. These *so-called* causal factors of culture, conditioning, genetics, etc. have a more original identity crisis.[110] Because of all the inconclusive data that overwhelmingly suggests a more common denominator as a cause of diverse behaviors, is it possible that the obviousness of the data being inclusive is obscure because of an ideological conditioning that refuses to look at the obvious. Complicating the results of information does make it difficult to see its nothingness.

If your reality is a conditioned view of selective perception, or said another way, a figment of your imagination projected in denial as an experience of a world untrue, then "mind over matter" is a true statement. As this body of a baby experiences its imagination of hunger, thirst, pleasure, pain, the mind that has limited itself to the identity of this projection must cope with the effects by making self-limiting mental adjustments. Because you believe you are a body, you experience as real the instincts of a body, the need for survival, and the development of this body's motor skills as well as a cognitive ability to make adjustments.[111] Naturally, this physiological/biological development of a

---

[110] In Kierkegaard's book *Sickness unto Death,* one's identity crisis was in relation to one's dis-relation with Source.
[111] This is the experience of what "mind over matter" is, as you limit your mind to the experience of matter.

predictable body process from birth to death could be viewed as life span stages. A cognitive adjustment does not understand true purpose about anything it looks upon when it has limited its view to the ever-changing. A developmental life span view of birth to death is a tempting substitution to frame ever-changing nothingness. Involved in a cycle of birth to death, you would erroneously justify social conditioning as being a meaningful cause.

Social conditioning is the process of adaptation; it is a constant mental shift to reinforce the belief that "you" as a body are the effect of an ever-changing body self-idea in a sea of interaction with other ever-changing body-self ideas. In short, social conditioning is an elusive cause of nothing with equally elusive and meaningless effects. The shift to identify with a body has been traditionally called an *egocentric* phase of child development.[112] More

---

[112] Developmental scientists are trying to move away from the language of an "egocentric" label. It's more popular to study early development as "interactive." Influenced by Jean Piaget's theory that development occurs in stages, in the mid 1960's American psychologist Lawrence Kohlberg (1927-1987) proposed a multistage theory of moral evolution. In the 1960s and 1970s British psychologist John Bowlby and American psychologist Mary Ainsworth introduced the concept of attachment. They proposed that infants and young children form emotional bonds to their caregivers because, throughout human evolutionary history, close attachments to adults promoted the survival of defenseless children. However, their parameters of why children behave the way they do has too many exceptions that do not justify the attachment theory as being consistently relevant. Bowlby and Ainsworth are not necessarily wrong as much as their studies about the effects of

accurately, the egocentric phase could be seen as a mind confused about what it thinks it is, adjusting as a body-centered shift out of a desire to identify with and find a home. As far as effects go, everything you think, do or say, involves the body as your center.[113] What you have been considering as causes, correlations and influences in your body life are actually all effects of a bigger cause. If "mind over matter" is a fact, then what you did is in self-deception. You have limited your experience to the life of a body and through the power of your mind to limit, you deny that you have done it to yourself.[114] That's why you constantly see the world wrong and then say it deceives you.

Do you believe you are a body because you experience a body? Or do you experience a body because you first believed yourself to be a body? Mind over matter suggests the later.

their theory can be generalized on a much larger scale than the limits their parameter of study permitted. To generalize everything: Grief, loss, need, hording, power, control, insecurity, war, ideology, anger, depression, fear, *the world of effects,* etc., from an attachment/abandonment point of view by not limiting it to the caregiver, invites the question: "Is there a simple content or dilemma we all share that is cause to the complexity of all these resulting forms?"

[113] *Symbols of Power p40*

[114] Denial comes in many hidden forms unrecognized like anger, guilt, fear, anxiety, depression, etc., to name a few of what all have as the same cause in common.

All these *so-called* causal factors of culture, conditioning, genetics, etc. are effects of a more original identity crisis. The obviousness of how overwhelmingly inconclusive all the data is, is obscured by a conditioned ideology that overlooks the obvious. "You" are not a body that is born to die through stages of development. Your resistance to know "you" beyond birth to death is more than just the effects of a social conditioning that limits you to deny "a something else" you already are. What does the data suggest?

News Flash!
This is just one news flash after another that fills our TV news and splashes all over our newspapers and computers on a daily basis.

> *August 1st 2013: Three teens are implicated in the killing of an elderly woman in her home for money. One of the teens who apparently orchestrated the robbery was the elderly woman's grandson.*[115]

Are you evolving? This is not just another bizarre isolated case of a legion of separate isolated cases that happen on a daily basis. Cosmetics of the world have changed nothing. One moment you can think that things are actually getting better and then the same day think it's all about ready to fall apart at the seams. Are you truly evolving or just imagining an evolution of progress through the ever-changing smoke and mirror? All these

---

[115] This example was randomly picked being reported on the day I was working on this section.

seemingly different forms hide a simple single content. Evolving information becomes irrelevant to the idea that each of us come into this journey with something specific to learn. And no matter what is going on around you, you have a particular task before you.[116] It does not have to be threatening to consider cultural, environmental, sociological, and nature factors as secondary or eventually irrelevant aids to your quest.

Since The Age of Enlightenment 350 years ago, human kind has been hopeful about a "New Age of Reason." However, no matter how enlightened you have become you still do all the things your ancestors did before and employ the same superstitious idols to justify all the destructive things your ancestors did before with the same denial your ancestors did before. I say *the same denial* because you want to selectively argue that things have gotten better in so many ways; while also selectively arguing as to how heinous or insane some acts of violence can be. If the right hand and left hand are kept separate from each other your mind can embrace its inconsistency. As I have said before, *if your mind seeks integration and a desire to protect a divided goal, for integrity sake it will deceive itself into believing that the conflicting goals are the same.* I would also add that your ego has just maneuvered subtly behind defending educational and technological achievements in the hope of showing you something remarkably progressive. The "New Age of Reason" continues with nothing new to show but the same show of nothing new that is seemingly different.

---

[116] *Symbols of Power p119-127*

Evolution is the illusion of trying to make the ever-changing look progressively meaningful. And conditioned thinking is the view that it is meaningfully progressive.

In spite of what you think, what really matters is what you are ready to learn when you are ready to learn it. This is a picture bigger than the imaginings of us all. The illusion of social and cultural learning has selective value when it helps you learn what your present task is to learn. Like when you teach your child to look both ways before crossing the street. There is something bigger than all the little crafty designs made up to measure learning accomplishment. Reality is not yours to select. What does the data suggest?

Summary

You did not begin when you were born to the body
You entered into an experience of distortion

Did you dream of incarnating out of guilt as a way of escaping the punishment you fear that guilt demands? This is the agenda you bring with you at birth. Because denial precedes projection, you forget this whole process. You may argue that social conditioning prevented you from knowing who you are, but you seem to be born because you don't know "The Self" you already are. Social conditioning and stages of development are but concepts, effects of not knowing "The Self" you already are. You know this is true because these concepts are intellectual paradigms made, as attempts to find out! The world and all its ideas attest to the fact that there is an unknown quality about "you" that already is, but can't be found in the world. Birth, infancy and childhood are part of the confusion that you think your innocence can be taken from you through a so-called conditioning.[117]

Though this process of developmental stages is generally and vaguely predictable, it is still individual, separate and unpredictable for each body. That this process is an effect that masks a greater cause is the real question. How we encountered being raised and socialized is not a cause of how we live our lives. How we live our lives is the manifestation of how we play through what we brought with us. This is a comment that transcends the duality of a nature verses nurture ideology. The dance between nature and nurture are but the effects of how we play our dilemma of alienation from "Being."

That social conditioning occurs is a given. That it is a cause of anything significant is a socially conditioned way of selectively perceiving and defending how your world-view occurred.

Social conditioning is not a cause of your confusion; it is an effect of already being confused.

Rethink this ideology. What does the data suggest?

---

[117] *Symbols of Power p123-124*

E. The Theory of Personality

Are you what you learn?
Are you organic?
Are you a combination?
Or are "you" before any of this came into play?

Introduction

Simply stated, personality has been considered as the sum of its parts.[118] But what those parts are is in dispute.

To most theorists, these parts are enduring patterns of thought, feeling, and behavior, which lends itself to some

---

[118] In Gestalt psychology, "The whole is *other* than the sum of its parts." In other words, the experience of your reality is not a *construction* of understanding the whole from the view of its seeming parts, but rather an *abstraction* of understanding the parts from the view of the whole. Gestalt psychology tries to understand the laws of our ability to acquire and maintain meaningful perceptions in a chaotic world. The central principle of Gestalt psychology is that the mind forms a global whole with self-organizing tendencies. This principle maintains that when the human mind (perceptual system) forms a percept or gestalt, the whole has a reality of its own, independent of the parts. The original famous phrase of Gestalt psychologist Kurt Koffka, "The whole is *other* than the sum of the parts" is often incorrectly translated as "The whole is greater than the sum of its parts" and thus used when explaining gestalt theory, and further incorrectly applied to systems theory. Koffka did not like the translation. He firmly corrected students who replaced "other" by "greater." "This is not a principle of addition" he said. The whole has an independent existence.

measure of predictability.[119] It is *assumed* that there are unconscious considerations of personality[120] as well as conscious and behavioral considerations for motivation with mixtures of all three for consideration as well as instinctual and or genetic considerations. Also, theorists emphasize different aspects of personality and disagree about its organization, development, and manifestation in behavior. In other words, there is little consensus as to what personality is and how to accurately measure what we don't know what "it is" we are talking about.

Personality can also be described existentially as the expression of an individual self as it relates to the world through a body. Blaise Pascal,[121] like later existential writers, saw human life in terms of paradoxes: The human self, which combines mind and body, is itself a paradox and contradiction. David Hume, a skeptic, denied the existence of the individual self, maintaining that because people do not have a constant perception of

---

[119] Personality tests (self-report and projective) depend on predictability or trends in personality. Although norms have been established to provide a comparative basis for interpreting a respondent's test scores, they are problematic because they lack predictability when it comes to a person's specific social context. The debate is currently around the importance of social context and individuality, and how these factors interact. Besides, to compare a score to a norm that is unknowable in the ephemeral is ludicrous.

[120] Freud and Jung found evidence for unconscious mental mechanisms of repression and resistance.

[121] Blaise Pascal (1623-1662) was a French philosopher, mathematician, and physicist; considered as one of the great minds in Western intellectual history.

themselves as distinct entities, they "are nothing but a bundle or collection of different perceptions." Albert Einstein[122] expressed that a man "experiences himself, his thoughts and feelings as something separate from the rest; a kind of optical delusion of his consciousness. This delusion is a kind of prison for us, restricting us to our personal desires ... Not to nourish the delusion but to try to overcome it is the way to reach the attainable measure of peace of mind." Buddha would not disagree with this.

With all this diversity of conflicting information, where is one to begin? Is there anyone out there?

Personality Development as a Theory

Are you so busy using measures to understand you that you do not understand that your measures limit you from understanding you?

To many theorists, the study of personality development is the study of one's process of integration and differentiation. Because observation is uniquely individual (subjective) and based on ephemeral (ever-changing) considerations, standards of measurement must be agreed upon in order to come up with professional consensus. In other words, quantitative bits of data are collected. Through a gentleman's agreement of subjective individualism and a "leap of faith," this

---

[122] Albert Einstein (1879-1955) was a German-born American physicist, best known as the creator of the special and general theories of relativity and for his hypothesis concerning the particle nature of light.

quantitative data becomes magically qualitative.[123] Can this approach tell you who or what you are?

Data may be collected and standardized, but it will mean what your tools are trained to conclude. Besides the fact that no one can decide what "it is" that is to be measured, what the data means is everybody's guess. Can what you are be understood through measured bits of data? Does complicating the results of information make it difficult to see its nothingness? Is there anyone out there?

Intelligence

Epistemology[124] as one of the main branches of philosophy is the study of "how" knowledge is derived. Can knowledge be derived from sense experience alone? Or, is it inherent to being? How is knowledge to be defined? To complicate the issue, is intelligence and knowledge the same thing?

Where does intelligence come from? As with any topic when it comes to the ephemeral, the debate over the nature - nurture paradigm rages endlessly. Within that paradigm, many scientists appeal to a common sense rather than a research sense that says: Intelligence is about half due to nature (heredity) and about half due to nurture (environment). Within that paradigm the experts say that the exact mechanisms by which genetic and environmental factors operate remain unknown. Beyond

---

[123] The magic of alchemy, smoke and mirrors

[124] Because epistemology is the field of study of how one "knows," it is once removed from experiencing knowing directly.

your memory, is there an inherent understanding that knows the experience of "being" beyond nature - nurture?

Some children are "naturally" more aware than others. Some children are more aware than adults. Though you may be involved in an adaptation towards learning developmental tasks, is your level of awareness a feature you brought with you on a journey to rise above sidetrack issues like nature vs. nurture? Beyond the empirical entanglement of complicating conflicting data, is there a level of awareness that depends on your karma or work you have already done?[125] You have heard "Out of the mouth of children comes wisdom." Before some children are socialized to think like the herd, they have an ability to fantasize and speak their mind, oblivious to social niceties. Is this just a matter of child-like naiveté or is there another level of awareness apart from any theory of personality development? Are our educational attempts to socialize a balance of conformity and creativity also the unknowing attempt to wash out any recollection[126] of the other side of the veil? "You can be creative," we are told, "as long as you create inside of the socially conventional box."

If you observe without ideology, you will find some children to be not curriculum smart, yet "other worldly" in awareness. Or, a child could have a high IQ (measured intelligence)[127] and lack practical awareness. Many children have achieved statesmen greatness in times of need and were not curriculum smart.[128] There is an

---

[125] *Symbols of Power p89*

[126] *Symbols of Power p111*

[127] Whatever that is?

[128] Abraham Lincoln, Sir Winston Churchill. This does hold the

awareness that is intangible to the microscope of endless degrees of measure[129] that transcends the designs of the empirical scientist.

René Descartes'[130] statement "I think, therefore I am" did not address what he was. The statement also assumes that thinking decides "being." One could just as easily state "I am … and when I think I get all confused about what I am." "Being" is cause before thought and thought is an effect of not knowing "Being Is" or "You Are." Descartes' missed the ride by putting the cart before the horse.

What exactly is intelligence? And this intelligence, that we don't know what it is or where it comes from, how is it to be measured? And why has all your learning through the perception of your world experience not given you the understanding as to how you learned what you learned through the ideological paradox of nature vs. nurture? Why is self-esteem a reoccurring issue for everyone who is born? Why have the great minds throughout the history of philosophy and psychology not

---

sacredness of curricular ideology as suspect to its real benefits.
[129] Testing for competency are markers that measure how well a child is being socialized.
[130] René Descartes (1596-1650) was a French philosopher, scientist, and mathematician, who is sometimes called the father of modern philosophy. Descartes determined to hold nothing true until he had established grounds for believing it true. The single sure fact from which his investigations began was expressed by him in the famous Latin words; Cogito, ergo sum, "I think, therefore I am." From this postulate that a clear consciousness of his thinking proved his own existence, he argued the existence of God.

figured it out? Like the existential writers before, the human self, which combines mind and body, is best understood as a paradox and contradiction. What does the data suggest? Is there anyone out there?

A motivation that wants to know has the potential for a transcendent experience of "Being"

Outcome Based

To teach is to demonstrate
To demonstrate is to teach
That is why teaching is one step away from knowing

Because learning is invisible, what has been learned is recognized by its results. Outcomes are forever inconclusive in all fields of study and education; curriculums are forever changing. What is new and innovative today will be old and deemed as falling short tomorrow. Does the old ideology of ever-changing outcomes demonstrate a flawed irrelevance of its ideology? Is there something in the way that keeps you from looking honestly at the ever-grinding ever-changing curriculums of change? Because you are measuring illusive inconclusive effects of nothingness, outcomes will always vary. They always have. Behavioral methods[131] of parenting and education cannot always be specific, relevant, immediate and consistent because consistency or stability is an illusion. This old worn out ideology is threatened by a different picture all together. What will

---

[131] *Symbols of Power p120-124*

be the next evolution of innovative smoke and mirrors to distract you from looking seriously at the last eight comments? It is erroneous to measure an evolution of awareness out of economic, technological and educational achievements.[132] Complexity of form does not imply complexity of content.

Outcome based results may demonstrate that the curriculum does what it says it will do (reliability factors) but the curriculum does not demonstrate usefulness if the outcome does not lend itself to peace of mind. This is not about doing therapy; this is about facilitating healing.[133] Is there anyone out there?

Self-Limiting Choices

Heraclitus said that the world is ever-changing and therefore demonstrates that stability cannot be found in the world. If the world is a demonstration of a lack of stability, then the only value the world has is that which would lead you out of the world. Everything else, being choices between illusive instability, would be meaningless.

To be lost in a sea of meaningless choices
And not know you are lost
Is to be lost indeed

---

[132] *Symbols of Power p84*
[133] *Symbols of Power p21-29*

Outcome-based education does not demonstrate merit if it does not recognize that what is being learned has a transcendent value. "Only infinite patience produces immediate effects"[134] is an example of practicing "infinite patience" for results that come out of a transcendent value. Can you wait for what will be to fall into its time and place? When you can, you will be in the time and place you need to be. This is a transcendent experience beyond the need to be in control of outcomes you can never be in control of. Your ability to generalize this learning to all other situations is a reinforcement that demonstrates that complexity of form does not imply complexity of content.

There is one simple content for you to choose among all the illusive ever-changing social circumstances you seem to experience. For example, if you cherish a concept of evil,[135] you will need to define it, show examples of evil and express why some behaviors/situations are motivated out of evil and why others are not the result of evil. One can easily say that Hitler, abortion, killing, capital punishment, lying, stealing, cheating etc. etc. etc. is evil. However, in the world of perception where certainty is illusive, not everyone agrees.[136] "I had to lie to my son to get him into treatment." "I stole bread because my children were starving." If for just a moment you suspend your belief about evil to see a particular instance in your life experience as a result of "ignorance"[137] rather than

---

[134] Gary Renard; *The Disappearance of the Universe p265*

[135] *The Way Home p63*

[136] How complicated do you want this conversation about external form to become?

[137] The word 'ignorance" is not an attempt to justify any act as

evil, and then generalized this lesson to everyone and everything you deem as negative or conflictual in your life, you would demonstrate that a complexity of many different forms has one simple content. Just like your mishaps, every perplexing event in your life experience can be explained as based on ignorance. You may have said many times "If I knew then what I know now, I would have done it differently." Don't get lost in the justification of comparing whose mistake is worse and whose is not as bad. Come to the understanding that ignorance is something we all have in common and your unwillingness to generalize it to all your perplexities of life events is common among us all. Either we are all hypocrites are none of us are. Simplifying motivation for peace of mind as the one content everyone has in common in their search for understanding allows you the *means* to experience peace of mind. Your endlessly frustrating reasons as to why people do what they do, dissolves into nothingness. Either you deny your confusion of ignorance temptingly looming, as your propensity to sabotage your journey to peace. Or you recognize in common your existential paradox, the human dilemma of contradiction, to be transcended. Which do you choose?

OK. It is an attempt for you to take a moment to look at the act differently. Some crimes are seen as so heinous that the word "evil" seems to be the ultimate word to describe it. Does that make it any less ignorant in the light of an ever-changing backdrop of total confusion that *you* in denial are also involved in? Socrates believed people were not willfully bad, just self-defeating out of ignorance.

There is a reason for all the lies
And that's the truth

You are a frustrated learner because your problem solving skills are limited to the rules of a limiting view. The belief you can find your bliss in the world of an ever-changing instability is a limiting view. Lest you become stupefied by the intelligence debate, you have unknowingly limited the power of your mind to fixed parameters of belief called an ideology. You are the victim or liberator of your own making. Frustrated learner, you can use the rules of your limiting view as a means to lead you beyond the rules themselves. Is there anyone out there?

Vulnerability with Identification

1) If purpose is meaning, and
2) If you identify yourself as a body, then
3) All meaning is derived from what you think the body is for.
4) If the body is a false identity then you do not know what anything is for.

Confusion about what you are is what the history of the world demonstrates. Endless wars, interpersonal boundary violations, verbal perceptions of impropriety since the dawn of written history, do not demonstrate awareness. All issues are around a body identity as a self you do not know. You either continue to deal with a dualistic contradiction of reason and impermanence. Or you are something other than your identity with a body all together.

To limit yourself to the expression of the body's senses, instincts and genetic disposition also limits you to being an object of change. You are born to experience pleasure, pain, failings, and achievements to suffer and die. You are vulnerable to fear, attack, pain and death. If you are not the body you have identified with then your mind has used the body as a means of deceiving itself.[138]

Body experiences are provoking distractions to the mind given over to them. Your mind is preoccupied with learning concepts and experiences through the activity, function and limiting distortion you personally identify with, called a body. This appears to attest to experiences of personal individuality.

> *Identification with the world is the making of an elusive*
> *"I" ego personality*
> *The idea of "desirability"[139] for the body is the form*
> *ego takes*
> *For "security" sake is ego's justification to live*
> *In the name of "happiness" is ego's cloak and dagger*
> *While "nothingness" is ego's reality*
> *Is there anyone out there?*

Identity Confusion

> *Projection makes perception*

---

[138] *Symbols of Power p144-150*
[139] value, purpose

Through fixed beliefs, perception stabilizes. So does a self-concept. What you perceive is a mirror of your state of mind, projected outward. What you are learning from and reacting to is your state of mind projected as a world, seemingly outside of and independent of you.[140] You project what you do not like and disassociate from recognizing that you projected it so you can be someone you are not. That is why all your dissatisfaction, unrest, contradiction, conflict, pleasure and pain, are experiences of confusion that teach you that you do not know what you think you are. "To despair over oneself, in despair to will to be rid of oneself--this is the formula for all despair"[141] is Kierkegaard's way of saying that to try to be who you are not is a rejection of self and the human condition of psychological alienation. Until you accept your conflictual contradictions as all coming from your projection you will empower blame as a real life justification and accept the never ending paradoxes that life seems to offer as a "you" in the process of becoming. The idea of finding a stable "self-esteem" in the "ever-changing becoming," is nothing more than an insane wish to establish a "you" that you are not in a place where meaning cannot be found.[142]

---

[140] Another way of saying it and not dependent on your awareness of it, is the fact that "karma is always instant." *Symbols of Power p90*

[141] *Sickness Unto Death* p 19. It is largely through this book and *The Concept of Anxiety* that Kierkegaard has been called the father of modern psychology.

[142] Heraclitus maintained that all things are in a state of continuous flux, that stability is an illusion.

Confusion of identity would cause you to search for meaning in a place it cannot be found. Your search for meaning in a place it can't be found demonstrates that you don't even know you have a confusion of identity that you are acting out. As far as your search for meaning goes, your purpose has gotten lost to a body identity of achievement and failure. Because confusion of identity breeds fear, your need to achieve takes any form that seems reasonable to the mind socialized to find a place of security and purpose in a world not its home. Frustration and fear are inevitable to the mind lost to the confusion of trying to find security and meaning in a place it can't be found. You seem to be socialized out of fear as Freud believed but not because the world is bad or wrong or insane or dysfunctional. You are socialized out of fear because you brought fear with you. The world is but your effect, the way you play out your fear. Simply stated; what you are learning from and reacting to is your state of mind looking back at you.

Only the insane continue to make what it fears, not realizing what it fears it made for itself to experience

Your attempts to blame your present life dilemma on life situations have not been successful for resolution. Though you can find superficial instances of conditioning,[143] the idea that you are a product of cultural conditioning solves nothing. You know this to be true because resolution eludes your grasp. Resolution eludes you because the cause of your dilemma does not come from

---

[143] Like prejudice and learning language

the world around you. Therefore, nor does your resolution come from the world. The world is your effect, the outcome of a confused mind. Look around you honestly, what in the world makes sense? You brought confusion of identity with you. Again, what you are learning from and reacting to is your state of mind reflecting back at you.

Your attempt to blame anything in the world is your attempt to deny that you are the cause of all the problems you see. And so it is, you unknowingly repeat the same relationship dysfunction over and over again with a seemingly different person, which makes it look like an altogether different problem. Is there an unconscious guilt that keeps you from looking at the obvious? You don't want to look at fear as your primary motivating factor for why you do what you do because who wants to experience fear? How else can you explain your denial of the obvious? You seem to be born ... as an effect of a more original error. Is there anyone out there?

Individuality

> As an aspect of my mind
> Together we walk in time
> Upon a thousand trails it seems
> Till we waken from the dream

> Matt Karayan
> The Last Dream

An aspect of a split mind is the fact that no one appears like another. There seem to be other individual personalities out there unknowingly sharing a dream of dancing to the pipers' musical spell. Individual points of view become unique according to the eye of each beholder. It is the dream of a collective hunch that tries to makes today's society seem cohesive through rules of exceptions and contradictions. However, it is merely an aspect of a mind split to unknowingly regard itself as subject and object. The denial of this split is the experience of a dream, sometimes a nightmare projected as those lost to the decision of their own dream. Your argued justifications for what you think you see, who you think you see and what you are doing, are your attempts to make your paradox of confusion about the meaningless dream make sense. You so badly want your projection of a world not true to be your home that you fight for the right to dance to the tune of a dirge out of tune.

To argue that you are an "individual" is not as justifyingly flattering as you think. It is the argument that you are "a one" of the innumerable ones that have come and gone and will continue on and on … endlessly. When you are shown over and over again that you are dispensable, the individual "you" wants to deny it and yet is easily hurt by the thought of it. Or is your seemingly "individual" birth an effect of a more original error?

> *Meaning is understood as shared*
> *Purpose is understood as shared*
> *Identity is understood as shared*[144]

---

[144] *Symbols of Power p101*

How can you defend your individuality while at the same time buy into the illusion of being a product of social conditioning and genetics? Neither concept can be in the awareness of your mind at the same time for they would demonstrate your contradiction of confusion about who you think you are! Your defense of "uniqueness" in the ever-changing is your insane wish to be an individual personality that can never be known, just assumed. It is you alone dreamer who decides what your dance means to you alone. It is also "You" that finds your identity in sharing the gifts you are.[145] Is there anyone out there?

Summary

There is an experience of "Being" before thought or conditioning that reminds you that "You already Are"

You seem to find identity in a temporary satisfaction of false security and pleasure. But it is always for a fleeting moment. That is why you are relentlessly driven to achieve a status you can never find.

Just for a present moment, clear your mind from all associations that seem to tell you what you think you are or should be. There is a "you" independent of genetic mannerisms, social conditioning,[146] job titles, money and family relationships. There is a "you" beyond a colorfully evolving process of ever-changing nothingness. But it will not be found alone because it will be experienced as shared.

---

[145] *Symbols of Power p133*
[146] *Symbols of Power p119-127*

To negate the irrelevant is to find what? What does the data suggest? Because nothing is known for sure, how could reality be yours to select? Your defense of your individuality is at the expense of knowing "You." Given the data, how do you explain your continued denial of the obvious? Is there anyone out there?

F. Economics Beyond Social Contracts

The philosophers have only interpreted the world in different ways. The point is to change it.

Karl Marx[147]

A Brief History of Political Philosophy

Political philosophy dates back to Plato and Aristotle who discussed the nature of the ideal government and the ideal society. It continued in theories on individual liberty and political institutions put forth by Hobbes, Mill, and Rousseau.

Aristotle had a view that "Man" is by nature a political animal because "Man" has the ability to communicate and dialogue about justice and the good. In Aristotle's view, it was natural for human kind to form social organizations of a political nature as a part of evolving, becoming.

Before the rediscovery of Aristotle it was believed by the church in the Middle Ages that government was a necessary evil. The Apostle Paul[148] believed that because of the sin of Adam[149] all things became corrupt.[150]

---

[147] Although Marx was a philosopher, he had disdain for merely theoretical intellectual work. His analysis of capitalist economy and the class struggle have become the basis of modern socialist doctrine.

[148] Paul, the Apostle (circa AD 3-62) was a self-proclaimed Apostle (1 Corinthians 9:1&2), who through the survival of his writings is considered the greatest missionary of Christianity and its first theologian.

[149] Romans 5; 12 & 19

There is none righteous, not even one
There is none who understands
There is none who seeks for God
All have turned aside
Together they have become useless
There is none who does good
There is not even one[151]

Thus it logically followed that government was a necessary evil.

Thomas Hobbes,[152] with a pessimistic view of human nature argued that humanity was doomed to conflict and chaos unless controlled by an exterior and overwhelming force. In contrast, democratic theorists such as John Locke believed in the essential goodness of people and argued that there was therefore no need for an all-powerful, absolutist government. Based on Locke's reasoning, Thomas Jefferson and other American thinkers wrote the Declaration of Independence and the Bill of Rights.

Politics in Action

Politics is but a substitution, an attempt to regulate the order of a kingdom on earth

---

[150] Genesis 3;17-19; Romans 8; 20-22
[151] Romans 3:10-12
[152] Thomas Hobbes (1588-1679) was an English philosopher and political theorist; one of the first modern Western thinkers to provide a secular justification for the political state.

NEWS FLASH!
September 26th, 2013
*The organization that led the charge to legalize
same-sex marriage in Minnesota is now under fire
for backing legislators who oppose abortion.*[153]

Today, political philosophy involves an energetic
dialogue between defenders of the liberal position and
defenders of the communitarian position. This dialogue is
played out through Ism's we call communism, socialism
and capitalism.

According to **Liberalism** the chief benefits of
government and society are personal and political
freedoms, such as freedom of speech, freedom of
association, and freedom of conscience (belief). Many
liberal theorists view the freedom to make moral choices
as the most important freedom; they argue that political
and social systems should be organized to allow
individuals the freedom to pursue their own ideas about
"the good life."

Communitarians respond that granting individuals
this extreme freedom of choice ultimately limits human
experience by undermining shared communal values.
They claim that by ignoring the importance of
community, liberalism disregards humanity's social
nature.

All this debate and conflict about "the ideal or most
practical government" is viewed by some as a breeding
ground for extreme views. **Anarchism** is a political theory
opposed to all forms of government. Anarchists believe

---

[153] Baird Helgeson / Star Tribune

that the highest attainment of humanity is the freedom of individuals to express themselves, unhindered by any form of repression or control from without. They hold that the perfection of humanity will not be attained until all government is abolished and each individual is left absolutely free. Purists of the cause state that one limitation on such freedom is the ban against injuring other human beings. From this limitation arises complication. From the anarchist view, if any human being attempts to injure others, all well-meaning individuals have the right to organize against him or her. The obvious problem with anarchism is that history demonstrates that humanity has not been able to live peaceably side-by-side; that righteous retaliation begets ... righteous retaliation.

Nihilism from the Latin word nihil meaning "nothing" has been applied to various radical philosophies (usually by their opponents). The implication is that adherents of these philosophies reject all positive values and believe in nothing. Most commonly, nihilism is presented in the form of existential nihilism, which argues that life is without objective meaning, purpose, or intrinsic value.

When the Master governs
The people are hardly aware that he exists
Next best is a leader who is loved
Next, one who is feared
The worst is one who is despised

Tao Te Ching #17

There is the Kingship of one, the regime of a few and the democracy of many. Each has their strong points; each has their flaws. Which do you choose? As always we end up with a mix of disagreeing confusion. Politics is a perfect example of duality at work ... nothing is for sure.

The Ethics of Politics and Law (excerpts)

Throw away holiness
and wisdom and people will be a hundred times happier
Throw away morality
and justice and people will do the right thing
Throw away industry and profit
and there won't be thieves

If these three aren't enough
Just stay in your center of the circle and let all things take
their course

Tao Te Ching #19

When the many decide who will represent the many, the few represent the many. When the few decide who will represent the many, the few represent the few in the name of the many. There is a corruption that comes from power.

The courts compile landmark cases upon cases ... to integrate the so-called "exceptional." Don't take it personally; it's just a game of chess.

Because the rules of politics were written by the incumbent, the rules of politics have an advantage to preserve the incumbent.

When you read a newspaper remember; it is a newspaper you are reading. Your real life is not in the content of the paper, but in the mind that made it.

Humor is a helpful perspective; it reminds you that there is always another point of view to anything.

Because political correctness curbs free speech, unbridled humor is the savior from the legislation of political correctness.

You can buy an expert to support any opinion you want.

Everybody wants fairness but nobody can clearly tell what it is.

Earth Politics

To you, who dream a walk upon the earth, listen;
Earth politics is not ecological legislation as it is ecological identification
It is not freedom fighters as it is fence burning
It is not housing authority as it is earth dwellers
It is not formal education as it is education beyond concrete walls
It is not just a clean-up to live respectful of Mother as it is a reflection of knowing the "self" you are

For the lesson of Earth politics asks; can I embrace my walk through with a dance of love, rhythm and rhyme and not get lost in its cycle?

Because your mind is split, the projection of duality reigns. Because duality reigns, politics becomes an effect of trying to bring order to what cannot be reconciled. As an effect, politics must reflect by following the trends of the majority, responding and reacting to the clamor of the minority or through coercion out of fear to stifle the unruly. That is why politics will not lead in world reform, but will follow the pressure of the trend. In the end, the pressure of the trend will be fed by the will of Mother ... and the will of Mother? The will of Mother Earth will take "all interests" and spew it out of her mouth! To the mind that does not know this, Mother will reclaim her own![154]

Business as Usual

I've had enough of reading things
By neurotic – psychotic – pig headed politicians
All I want is the truth, just gimme' some truth
No shorthaired–yellow-bellied son of tricky dicky[155]
Is gonna' mother hubbard soft soap me
With just a pocket full of hope
Money for dope; money for rope

John Lennon
Gimme' Some Truth

---

[154] *Symbols of Power p43-52*
[155] Referring to President Richard Nixon in 1971

You may want to scream "All I want is the truth, just gimme' some truth!" But what is the truth?" The corporate boss might say, "The one in charge knows." The worker might say, "The collective masses know." The individual might say, "I know." The existentialist might say, "No one knows." The ethicists might say, "It depends upon the context." The utilitarian might say, "That which serves the greatest good." The nihilist might say, "There is no truth." So, what is the truth?

The current business paradigm is as old as the hills. Power resides at the top; it is not shared. Because of this, decisions of policy, problem solving and communication flow from the top down. To Thomas Hobbes who had a pessimistic view of human nature, power at the top is more efficient than shared power. However, because the worker is a recipient of policy rather than an active participant they may not feel empowered and can feel disgruntled. In this light, the worker is not always willing to be a participant because they are not invested in a common purpose. Mediocrity and lack of motivation are symptoms of lack of common purpose. Job dissatisfaction and boredom flourish. It also breeds professional jealousies between the haves and have not's.

Professional jealousy makes other people crazy
When they think you've got something that they don't have
What they don't understand is it's just not easy
To cover it all and stand where you stand
Professional jealousy makes no exception
It can happen to anyone at any time
The only requirement is knowing what's needed
And then delivering what's needed on time

Van Morrison
Professional Jealousy

Those who are not committed to *their own single purpose* will project dissatisfaction.

Empowering Dependence[156]

The more subsidies you have
The less self-reliant people will be

Tao Te Ching #57

We teach our children to "empower" themselves within an economic consumer vacuum of dependence. "Don't you dare question 'the fact' that I need my cell phone and a car to survive!" How can you ask anyone to change what they have become accustom to believing they "need?" To make a living, we are reinforcing the conditioning of excelling within a limiting paradigm of

---

[156] "Empowering dependence" is a self-defeating contradiction of words.

dependence. We live within a social paradox of technological advances that sabotage. You think you need your TV to find out what is going on in the world when the entire world is going on in your mind.

"Evolve, be creative" you are told, "As long as you only think within the box of how things are to work," is the whisper; because anything outside the box is a threat to a social order that is working hard to deny the chaos that is swirling around it. It is self-deception to believe that economic development is evolving creation, freedom and progress. Economic development is not bad or wrong, it is just one of the many substitutions to mask a mind split in a battle. Look at what was once a luxury; now it's an adjusted lifestyle of "necessity."

The science that has made survival for the body comfortable is an addiction to the mind that has adjusted to depend on it

I nickel and dime for things each day
"But I need things to satisfy" I say
So I collect thoughts and images to fill spaces in my mind
In an attempt to drive present moments out of time
And because I a-mass for a satisfaction that does not last
I nickel and dime myself each day

Even still, in the light of karma (the effects of a split mind) none of this matters.[157]

---

[157] *Symbols of Power p89-105*

The New Economics

I can work with what you offer because it fits with my purpose

The New Economics is not a form of Marxian ideology or capitalism; none of which is practiced purely anyway. This New Economics does not thrive within a stock market ideological "confidence." It is not symbolized by green slips of numbered papers and different sized shiny metal disks.[158]

It's not what the world holds for you that makes a difference. It's what you bring to the world that makes all the difference in the world.

The New Economics is an experience from within; it is an experience beyond words. The New Economics is a satisfaction that makes external recognition of accomplishment irrelevant. To be passionate about your own purpose as already shared beyond consumer products of supply and demand is the New Economics. The New Economics is an experience of purpose and well-being that swells from within ... beyond ego identity ... beyond recognition ... as expressed through love.

Fill your bowl to the brim and it will spill
Keep sharpening your knife and it will blunt
Chase after money and security and your heart will never unclench

---

[158] *The Way Home p152-154*

Care about people's approval and you will be their prisoner

Do your work, then step back
The only path to serenity

Tao Te Ching #9

Within the old paradigm was exploitation of the proletariat. Whatever the business paradigm might be is irrelevant to the New Economics because the New Economics has a purpose from *within* that involves an attitude of transcendence. How can you be exploited when you are a passerby? When you do whatever you do for the joy of it, everything else follows. This New Economics is not new. It's older than the hills.

Summary

I can walk with you if you are going my way

Many want to see economics as a social contract, an equal distribution of wealth (whatever that means) to be shared fairly through political legislation. Others see the rights of individual labor as being the fair measure of reward. Because of the conflict of a split mind projected as political and economic debate, the best you can do to live within that conflict is to strive for balance. Because nothing is definitive, fairness is forever fleeting. Greed, envy, wealth, poverty, power and oppression are the absolutes of fairness your mind demands through its identity with a body as itself. Even still, it is but a state of mind.

The Master has no possessions
The more he does for others the happier he is
The more he gives to others the wealthier he is

Tao Te Ching #81

As the stock market teaches, everything is in a constant state of flux and flow; unfolding and constricting. What is definitive in economics, politics and law? What do you want to make it mean? What does the data suggest? Is reality yours to select?

Be content with what you have
Rejoice in the way things are
When you realize there is nothing lacking
The whole world belongs to you

Tao Te Ching #44

G. Confusion's Clash

War is a demonstration of minds acting out their confusion through bodies

Introduction

Because history demonstrates that war has been a way of life, either war is a way of life or life as you know it is INSANE

From the dawn of this civilization,[159] conflict has always been part of the human condition. If the integration of a single purpose "What is my bliss?" has been your primary motivating factor, it has eluded you since the beginning of time. How is one to explain humanity's reason for being unable to live in peace?

St Augustine,[160] in an attempt to reconcile the teachings of Christ with the reality of a world of war was one of the first to assert that a Christian could be a soldier and serve God and country honorably. He claimed that,

---

[159] Don't assume there has not been a civilization of intelligence before this civilization's dawn. *Symbols of Power p83-85*

[160] Augustine of Hippo (354–430), was an early Christian theologian and philosopher whose writings influenced the development of Western Christianity and Western philosophy When the Western Roman Empire began to disintegrate, Augustine developed the concept of the Catholic Church as a spiritual City of God, distinct from the material Earthly City. His thoughts profoundly influenced the medieval worldview.

while individuals should not resort immediately to violence, God has given the sword to government for good reason.[161]

Arthur Schopenhauer,[162] not well received in his time because of his seeming pessimism, was convinced that human history was going nowhere. After two World Wars that put a damper on 19th century anticipations of evolving progress[163] that had captured the hearts of thinkers such as Hegel and Marx, Schopenhauer's writings became significant within 20th century philosophy.

Unquestionably, war is a demonstration of individual minds acting out their confusion through bodies. Because

---

[161] Based upon Romans 13:4; As a doctrine, the purpose of the **Just War Theory** is to ensure that war is morally justifiable through a series of criteria, all of which must be met for a war to be considered just. Just War Theory postulates that war, while very terrible, is not always the worst option. There may be responsibilities so important, atrocities that can be prevented or outcomes so undesirable to justify war.

[162] Among 19th century philosophers who wanted to believe that world consciousness was evolving in awareness, Arthur Schopenhauer the seeming pessimist was among the first to contend that at its core, the universe is not a rational place.

[163] German idealism was a philosophical movement in Germany in the late 18th and early 19th centuries. It developed out of the work of Immanuel Kant in the 1780s and 1790s, and was closely linked both with romanticism and the revolutionary politics of the Enlightenment. The most well-known thinkers in the movement were Immanuel Kant, Johann Gottlieb Fichte, Friedrich Schelling, and Georg Wilhelm Friedrich Hegel. Simply stated, they wanted to believe that world consciousness was evolving in awareness.

complexity of form does not imply complexity of content, from the view of a single content, war as a demonstration of confusion is the effect of a mind split, divided against itself and projected into innumerable forms. Again and unquestionably all these forms of battle, conflict, war, arguing and misunderstandings are the commonality of a mind confused about itself. It is truly amazing that any semblance of the exchange of meaning occurs.

Plato's Cave

According to Plato, in the world of form all you are doing is reacting to shadows. The Allegory of the Cave depicts individuals as chained deep within the recesses of a cave.[164] Bound so vision is restricted (bound to perception), they cannot see one another. The only thing visible is the wall of the cave upon which appear shadows cast by the individuals chained to look only at the wall. Cast by a fire behind them, it is their own shadow they are reacting to as real. Breaking free, one of the individuals escapes from the cave into the light of day. With the aid of the sun, that person sees for the first time the real world and returns to the cave with the message that the only things they have seen are shadows and appearances and that the real world awaits them if they are willing to struggle free of their bonds.

The shadowy environment of the cave symbolizes the physical world of appearances. Escape into the sun-filled setting outside the cave symbolizes the transition to the real world, the world of full and perfect knowing.

---

[164] The Republic is structured as a fictional dialogue between Socrates and Glaucon, two Greek thinkers.

However, those bound to see only the wall of shadows resist the idea that there is something more than what they experience through perceiving. The idea of thinking outside of their box of beliefs is threatening to the limits they have acclimatized themselves to live with.

According to the allegory, man's condition is one of bondage to fixed beliefs, perceptions of conditioned thinking. Thinking that "Only what is real is what I see" you unknowingly justify what you perceive as what is "real" not realizing you perceive only what you ask to see within the limits of your conditioned thinking. The existentialists would see it as the mass mentality of the many not willing to think independently of the herd. You think you think independently as the experience of an "individual" as you follow along in the herd of "individual" thinkers chained to the perception of selective beliefs. It is truly amazing that any semblance of the exchange of meaning occurs.

The Confusion of Communication

Because perception brings your mind into the arena of uncertainty, the arena of a world ever-changing, it is "only you" that makes the world mean anything you want it to mean. Is there anybody out there?

Meta-communication is conversation about how communication works. That a word can seem to kill or heal is vulnerability; but only to a mind that thinks it is a body. It is your mind that assesses danger.[165]

---

[165] Startle reaction is an involuntary response to sudden,

Hearing another's words does not make you a good listener when you unknowingly and all too easily put your own spin to the sounds of someone you think is out there. William James said that all concepts are changeable and depend on the context in which they are being discussed. Plato believed that anything involving perception and change would be imperfect. Appearances are deceiving when they are only appearances you refuse to acknowledge. Specifically, you are not reacting to another's words as much as you are reacting to your own interpretation of another's words. Because you are *never* angry or hurt for the reason you think, your anger and hurt *always* demonstrates this fact.

When you *react* to another's ignorance as something personally real, you are unknowingly reacting to your own shadow of ignorance by not seeing theirs for what it is. You cannot know for sure what it is you are reacting to in the darkness of a cave, in the whirlwind of a hurricane, in the ever-changing world you think is real when you can't see that that is what everybody else is doing.

Throughout the history of the world, alliances and truces have been continuously made only to be broken out of misunderstanding, ignorance and of course fear. Meaning exchanged between bodies in an elusively ever-changing world context makes society a collective hunch. It is a wonder that any semblance of the exchange of meaning occurs.

startling stimuli, such as sudden noise or sharp movement. Traditionally it was viewed as an unconscious neurological reflex for the body's survival.

The War of the Words

Sticks and stones may break my bones
But words can never hurt me

Anonymous

Litigation is the means for the resolution of misunderstandings. Arbitration is the norm. How could this be in the 21st century when all the information you need for *clarity and awareness* is at your fingertips? Education for equality, personal freedom and fairness as a solution is the pervasive measure to fix that which would be construed as offensive. And yet, we make righteous the justification for wars that kill others. We are even more polite in waging wars with words that don't kill bodies to hide the fact that it is minds that kill bodies, not bodies that kill bodies. Meaning is elusively ever-changing.

It is a thought that kills or frees
The body is just its messenger

The landscape of the battlefield is ever-changing while the battle continues to rage on. Meaningful solutions to the problems in the world at the level of interaction between bodies remain elusive. The Age of Enlightenment that started 350 years ago is no further along. However, solutions are meaningful when they transcend the confusion of the clash of bodies. In other words, meaningful solutions are not to be found in the world because the world was made for you to look but not find.

Two men looking through jail house bars
One sees mud, the other sees stars

God on Our Side

Verse 1: *My name it is nothin' ... My age it means less*
The country I come from ... Is called the Midwest
I's taught and brought up there ... The laws to abide
And that the land that I live in ... Has God on its side

Verse 9: *So now as I'm leavin' ... I'm weary as Hell*
The confusion I'm feelin' ... Ain't no tongue can tell
The words fill my head ... And fall to the floor
If God's on our side ... He'll stop the next war

Bob Dylan
With God on Our Side

I can't venture to guess how many wars have been fought in the name of a loving God. The need to defend a religious righteousness involves a fictional belief in a lovingly wrathful God to compensate by punishing the unrighteous. The unrighteous would be the ones who do not share your view of what God like righteousness looks like. It is important here that the right hand does not know what the left hand is thinking lest the insanity of one's logic should be revealed. Nietzsche stated that "All things are subject to interpretation. Whichever interpretation prevails at a given time is a function of power and not truth."[166]

Kill one man and you're a murderer
Kill a million and you're a conqueror

Jean Rostand

It is truly amazing that any semblance of the exchange of meaning occurs.

Confusion's Religious Clash

Blaise Pascal, in his *Pensées* (1670) expressed that a systematic philosophy that presumes to explain God and humanity, is a form of pride. The arena of diverse theological views presuming what God is about is what all the different denominational views, within all the different religions of the world, are about. Which view about God and how to live a righteous life is the right one? The fact that no one group is entirely consistent with what to believe about God and how to live the "righteous life," is problematic in itself. Besides the fact that different religions abound because of different beliefs about God, we also have self-proclaimed orthodox beliefs calling other beliefs cultic in nature. Then there are religious views that on one hand abhor paganism or polytheism in the name of a monotheistic[167] belief in God, while on the

---

[166] The Orthodox or "right view" is the view that wins out over the other. That is exactly what happened at The First Council of Nicaea in 325 AD when they formed the Canon of the New Testament.

[167] Meaning that there is only one God

other hand worship at the crucifixion of their savior, crucified for the shedding of blood by his own loving father to appease his vengeful wrath for a fallen nature that He himself put into motion.[168] And every person who has read this sacred text has their own interpretation of this event different than any other. What does all of this mean? What are you to believe? Only the confusion of a split mind through magical thinking could allow for this conflict of a logic that could never be.

Is it a cruel God that justifies the right for His own creation to kill each other? Is it an insane God that allows rape, murder, thievery of the disadvantaged and pure of heart and lying to slander another? Did God abandon His children to teach them a lesson? Do you only focus on a God of love to avoid the contradiction of a split mind for an eventual piece of pie in the sky? Is this planet a psycho-planet made by a wrathfully loving God? "Something must be done!" the madman exclaims.[169]

God is dead. God remains dead. And we have killed him. Yet his shadow still looms. How shall we comfort ourselves, the murderers of all murderers? What was holiest and mightiest of all that the world has yet owned has bled to death under our knives: who will wipe this blood off us? What water is there for us to clean ourselves? What festivals of atonement, what sacred games shall we have to invent? Is not the greatness of this deed

---

[168] Your concept of God is a projection of your guilt, if you think you can oppose the will of God and succeed. Only a God that punishes for salvation's sake will be your effect.

[169] In fairness to Nietzsche, this is the context he writes from.

too great for us? Must we ourselves not become gods simply to appear worthy of it?

Friedrich Wilhelm Nietzsche
The Gay Science, Section 125

In the light of a complex paradoxical conflicting religious presentation of a wrathfully loving God, a "God is dead" approach to life seems reasonable. Religions have given people a reason to be atheists.

When they lose their sense of awe, people turn to religion. When they no longer trust themselves they begin to depend on authority

Tao Te Ching #72

In response, Karl Jaspers[170] rejected explicit religious doctrines; beliefs that limit ones experience of Being. Rather, he was preoccupied with transcendence and the limits of human experience.

Within the confusion of a magical logic that human kind communicates out of, it is truly amazing that any semblance of the exchange of meaning occurs. Communicating for a unified religion is impossible. It is a shared experience of "Being" that is waiting for us all. What does the data suggest?

---

[170] Karl Jaspers (1883-1969) was a German philosopher, one of the originators of existentialism, whose work influenced modern theology, psychiatry and philosophy.

Isms of Confusion

Everybody's talkin' bout' Bag-ism, Shag-ism, Drag-ism, Mad-ism, Rag-ism, Tag-ism, This-ism, That-ism, isn't it the most?
All we are saying is give peace a chance

John Lennon
Give Peace A Chance

It is obvious that battle in all its forms is the dizziness of separate minds acting out their confusion through bodies.

Nationalism,[171] under the colors of different flags, is the alliance of separate minds cloaked in the name of "Truth, Justice, Freedom and what I think is right." Nationalism as a reason for freedom has always been a justification for war.[172] Nationalism is a crafty way to justify the accumulation of an army of collective confusion to secure body space. Weapons become devices used by a body in an attempt to expand mind's policy of confusion on a massive scale.

Libertarianism[173] vs. **Collectivism**[174] are superficial labels to hide a deeper human dilemma of being. No

---

[171] Nationalism is a sense of consciousness exalting one nation above all others and placing primary emphasis on the promotion of its culture and interests as opposed to those of other nations or supranational groups
[172] Both World War I & II attest to this.
[173] Libertarianism is the political philosophy emphasizing the rights of the individual over government rule. The doctrine of libertarianism stresses the right to self-ownership and, by

matter how you frame the vacilation of political confusion, it is simply a never-ending demonstration of duality's battle in your mind. Your defense of your ideology is a way to not see the confusion you are advocating.

They say that patriotism is the last refuge
To which a scoundrel clings
Steal a little and they throw you in jail
Steal a lot and they make you king
There's only one step down from here babe
It's called the land of permanent bliss
What's a sweetheart like you
Doing in a dump like this?

Bob Dylan
Sweetheart Like You

I am not saying you should not defend the illusion of your individual liberties. I am asking if you have to be crazy to be a serious player in the understanding of world affairs. The bigger picture continually suggests that you will not find meaning in the world because the world was made to deny you meaning. This is what the data of our

---

extension, the right to private ownership of material resources and property. Advocates oppose any form of taxation and the growth of the state over individual rights.
[174] Collectivism is a term used to denote a political or economic system in which the means of production and the distribution of goods and services are controlled by the people as a group. Generally this refers to the state. Collectivism is the opposite of capitalism or free enterprise.

history constantly suggests. It is truly amazing that any semblance of the exchange of meaning occurs.

Hypocrite

The world is a mental paradox of dualistic ambiguity. There are innumerable mental contradictions you find yourself in as being "damned if you do and damned if you don't." No one's behavior can live up to their own words. You are inconsistent with thinking as well as being inconsistent with the follow through (behaviors) of inconsistent thinking. That's why misunderstanding is legion on a personal as well as global scale. And because appearances are deceiving you are predisposed to interpret another's motive in self-hurting ways ... and blame them for it. When words are released they seem to have a power all to them self.

You don't have control over how another will interpret your words. But you do have power over *your interpretation* of another's words. This is a battleground that is different than the killing of bodies. It is a battle for your mind!

In a soldier stance I aimed my hand at the mongrel dogs who teach
Fearing not I'd become my enemy in the moment that I preach

Bob Dylan
My Back Pages

133

That we are all hypocrites is one way to look at the world. And if you choose to look for inconsistency, you will perceive it in everything and everybody. Another way to look at the world is instead of being a hypocrite because you do not consistently follow through with what you say, rather, it is that you teach what you need to learn because you do not always follow through with what you say. This is an example of a non-dualistic principle that leads your mind beyond the confusion of your dualistic world-view. This is because it is a self-forgiving, non-dualistic, unifying interpretation of understanding motives and thus behavior. Not just your motive and behavior but everyone's! Everyone is teaching what they need to learn because they need to learn it.[175] You cannot accept forgiveness for your lack of consistency until you recognize it in everyone you meet. If you do not recognize yourself in everyone you meet, you will accuse them of being the hypocrite you refuse to see in yourself. When you identify with another beyond any "ism" you will be able to throw the word "hypocrite" away for good. Either reality is not yours to select because it is shared as One, or the hypocrite you see in the world will always be a projection of what you do not want to see in you.

Another example that allows your mind to transcend the mind–body (eternal-temporal paradox) contradiction your mind is tempted to perceive is to tell yourself,

---

[175] Out of ignorance many teach confusion. Trying to teach impossible lessons is what makes one a poor teacher. This is the making of the frustrated learner. *Symbols of Power p98-105*

To attempt to be perfect in terms of behavior is self-defeating. All that is necessary is a willingness to receive direction.

This comment is an example of a non-dualistic focus for a unified goal for peace of mind because it transcends the conflict of any contradiction (duality) your mind is tempted to perceive. Otherwise, it is truly amazing that any semblance of the exchange of meaning occurs.

Idolized Truth

Change it had to come – We knew it all along
We were liberated from the fall – that's all
But the world looks just the same
And history ain't changed
Cause the banners, they all flown in the last war
And I'll get on my knees and pray
We don't get fooled again

The Who
Won't Get Fooled Again

It is often said and *idolized as truth* that we should learn from our past so we don't repeat it. However, the one thing the past teaches is that we don't learn from it.[176] We hand down the same old worn out problems to the next generation ... just packaged in another unrecognizable form to be solved again. This is what the data screams.

---

[176] *Symbols of Power p83-85*

To perceive another only as you see them NOW makes their past irrelevant in the present. Your past reaction to him would also not be present. You would only respond to him as he is NOW. To react to a memory of him in the present would be to not have a meaningful exchange with him because you would not be interacting with him as he is NOW. Have you been trying to learn an impossible lesson from the past that perpetuates the past in the future, negating the present? It is amazing that any semblance of the exchange of meaning occurs.

A Tailor is one who sizes every person anew each time he meets them. Be a Tailor

Another phrase of *idolized truth* is "I'll forgive him but never forget." Besides the fact that this phrase has nothing to do with forgiveness, it is insane to perceive what "was" in place of NOW and yet say you forgive. To bring the past into the present is to communicate through a cherished illusion, the memory of your perception of the other rather than to talk with who he is NOW.

Paradoxically, we teach each other to learn from the past so you do not repeat your mistakes. Yet, the world is continually being forged out of an original mistake. The world is a place where meaning cannot be found. Repeat offenses, prisons and wars are just a few demonstrations of our inability to learn from the consequences of our past. The one thing we need to learn from the past is not that we don't learn from the past but that we don't learn from the past because it is not real! It is truly amazing that any semblance of communication occurs.

Meet the new boss
Same as the old boss

The Who
Won't Get Fooled Again

Summary

The more weapons you have, the less secure people will be

Tao Te Ching #57

What one can conclude in the midst of all this communication of confusion is that the clash of bodies is a witness to a world in perpetual confusion. Negotiation for peace has been from the dawn of this civilization. However, instead of learning community and wholeness as one would think on an evolving scale, is the continuation of loss, separation, alliances, betrayal and fear that is exchanged, but never shared. Peace at the level of bodies seems temporarily fragile at best and always elusive. Because perception brings us into the arena of uncertainty, all *so-called reality* is constantly being negotiated. And as a problem solving technique, violence is highly overrated ... especially when it perpetuates itself. Meaningful solutions to the problems in the world are not to be found at the level of interaction between bodies. They are realized as shared in experience when they transcend the confusion of the clash of bodies. Peace between bodies is the effect of a shared experience of One mind.[177]

---

[177] *The Way Home p115-119*

After the game, the King and the Pawn go into the same box

Italian proverb

Though bodies clash, its true meaning seems to be hidden by the appearance of the clash itself. What does the appearance of the clash of bodies represent? That war and conflict is a demonstration of minds' acting out their confusion through bodies. The common factor is a mind split, divided and therefore confused about what it is.

Your clash of confusion justifies a nationalized defense of pride (an alliance of egos) around your little kingdom. This diversion prevents you from your opportunity to recognize you in everyone you meet as your passage through. Because we are aspects of the confusion of a split mind, we will join through its healing. That is the only thing time is for.

Now he's hell-bent for destruction
He's afraid and confused
And his brain has been mismanaged with great skill
All he believes are his eyes
And his eyes, they just tell him lies
But there's a woman on my block
Sitting there in a cold chill
She say who gonna' take away his license to kill

Bob Dylan
License to Kill

An obvious question regarding the history of human kind: why don't we learn what we need to learn from war? Given the data, how do you explain your continued denial of the obvious?

H. The Concept of Disease

Not knowing is true knowledge
Presuming to know is a disease
First realize that you are sick
Then you can move toward health
The Master is her own physician
She has healed herself of all knowing
Thus she is truly whole

Tao Te Ching #71

Introduction

Plato suggested that you gave your mind over to a body of change, became charmed by its shadow dance and lost to its process. Your experience of this unnatural association leads you to descriptions of this process. The ideas of etiology (cause), pathology (process) and prognosis (predicted outcome) are descriptions of a process.[178] To diagnose is to identify where someone is at in their process through the symptoms they present. The process they describe is that of your body.[179]

Apart from the fact that all organisms proceed towards ever-changing fragmentation, for our purposes we will define the word disease as *"any deviation from or interruption of the normal structure or function of any body part, organ, or system that is manifested by a set of*

---

[178] Theories of lifespan development also describe a process
[179] Body includes brain physiology, not mind. *Symbols of Power p31-42*

symptoms and signs and whose etiology, pathology, and prognosis may be known or unknown."[180]

Mind Beyond Time

Is there really a choice?
Or does your path choose you?

Most theorists *assume* that everything that goes on between birth and death is up to physiological developmental successive approximations of varying psychological influences that present predictable possibilities with unpredictable twists of fate. Within this paradigm some assume an evolution that "has its reasons."[181] But it is just another spin to justify or make *purposefully meaningful,* physiological developmental successive approximations of varying psychological influences that present predictable possibilities with unpredictable twists of fate.[182] Simply stated:

> *Fate takes one where one goes*
> *The others it drags along*

Roman Proverb

Heraclitus suggested that everything you experience, including the body, is in a process of constant change. The idea of stability is an illusion. Death after birth is predictably perfect, but nothing else is. To be born, get

---

[180] The Free Dictionary
[181] *The Way Home p68, Symbols of Power p119-127*
[182] Pseudo-Synchronicity: *Symbols of Power p46*

personally involved in a life; go to school, find a job, get married, have children, pay taxes, save money to comfortably retire; in short, build your little kingdom, and then POOF! ... you're gone ... is an incomprehensible intangibility to the one digging in. The existentialists will tell you that your joy over birth and grief over death is the witness to your investment in and denial of this ultimate absurd paradox.

Because evolution is an illusion of conditioned thinking:

1. To see progress in the ever-changing spin is self-deception.

2. Not being aware of this circular process of nothingness is your illness.

3. Trying to make all this nothingness meaningful is your means to remain ill.

So, and as it seems, in the ephemeral of an ever-changing world, all outcomes are ever-changing, always seemingly becoming, as the demonstration of the illusion of evolution. Through this lens, all your choices are between random happenings that have nothing to do with meaningful outcomes. But if you look closely through the veil of ever-changing appearances, you will find an outcome that is already accomplished for and by you. This is your experience of Mind beyond time.

The "Unexamined Self"

Through your association with a body you experience pain and pleasure, yet always fleeting. You experience love and fear of which both seem to be fleeting. You maneuver for security sake and remain anxious. All your decisions are around a body of process where ultimate outcomes do not belong to you.[183]

Existentially speaking, you may want to be eternal and yet experience the cycle of temporal change. This is what Kierkegaard calls "the absurdity of being;" an anxiety you cannot escape. Either you grasp this dilemma head on or bury it alive … as unconscious. Your denial of this dilemma is the cause of your psychological ailments. It is to live an inauthentic life. This "unexamined self" is like Socrates' "unexamined life." Living "as if" is not living "as is." Based on his study of Immanuel Kant, Friedrich Nietzsche and Jeremy Bentham's Theory of Fictions, Hans Vaihinger's philosophy[184] holds that while sensations and feelings are real, the rest of human knowledge consists of "fictions" that can only be justified pragmatically or in Nietzsche's words can be "useful fictions." Vaihinger argued that human beings can never really know the underlying reality of the world and that as a result we construct systems of thought and then assume that these match reality: we behave "as if" the world matches our models. For example: Many people behave as if there were a heaven or a hell in their personal future. And they selectively perceive people, places and things in a way to reinforce this belief. There may be a heaven or a hell, but most of us don't think of this as a proven fact. That makes

---

[183] *Symbols of Power p39-40*
[184] Hans Vaihinger (pronounced: häns fihing-r) (1852-1933) was a German philosopher whose system of thought was set forth in 1911 as The Philosophy of "As If" and was translated into English in 1924 as *The Philosophy of 'As If': A System of the Theoretical, Practical and Religious Fictions of Mankind.*

it a "fiction" in Vaihinger's and Adler's sense of the word. Alfred Adler[185] added that, "at the center of each of our lifestyles, there sits one of these fictions, an important one about who we are and where we are going." In short, we live according to defended beliefs that have nothing to do with "Being."

Your decisions are about your body; either to attain pleasure, satisfaction or to avoid pain and fear is not a "useful fiction." Your *not-obvious* addiction to and defense of a body-self idea as your personal center of safety (which will fail you), is the making of and reason for your fear. As far as your safe haven of identity goes, your body is continually progressing towards an ever-changing fragmentation of what the earth does. While giving intellectual consent to others as you drive by a cemetery, your denial of this "fiction" as your body's process is an underlying fear that causes you to bury alive the obvious. Given the data, how do you explain your continued denial of the obvious paradigm of cause, process and outcome that predicts the demise of everything you hold dear? "I don't have time to think about my inevitable future," you argue. "I have to secure for tomorrow!" The eternal and temporal is a paradox continually knocking on your door to tell you to live in the NOW, yet plan for a future that is

---

[185] Alfred W. Adler (1870–1937) was an Austrian medical doctor, psychotherapist, and founder of the school of individual psychology who emphasized the importance of feelings of inferiority; the inferiority complex as an element which plays a key role in personality development. Adler was the first to emphasize the importance of the social re-adjustment process in child development. Alfred Adler was greatly influenced by Vaihinger and Nietzsche.

unsure out of a past that isn't. "I can't afford to look at the paradigm of process that comes with the 'fiction' of associating with a body," you tell yourself.

With all this complexity of form, to survive is to live "as if;" the "unexamined self."

The Paradigm of Process

If healing is of the body
Then healing is not real
Because the body dies

It rains, evaporates into vapor and condenses into rain is a fact of the ephemeral. Whether you perceive it or not, everything is involved in a circular process of change. The body you think you are is a part of this process. Within the paradigm of cause, process and predicted outcome is disease, degeneration and death explained as a process. What this process of change means is an assumption or "fiction" based on what you believe you are.

Your experience of disease, degeneration and death comes out of your belief that the body you experience as "what you are" is your personal center of operation. The power of your mind is such that it will experience the deceptions you choose it to associate with. In other words, what you select to believe you will experience as true for you and you will selectively perceive only those witnesses to justify the experience of what your mind first selected to believe.[186]

---

[186] Your mind is too fragmented to be able to practice mind over matter consistently.

Every addiction builds an environment that will defend the addiction. Even though a fragmented world was made out of a fragmented mind, your mind's addiction to a fragmenting body image as itself is defended as justified for survival sake, because of all the environmental assailants that are fragmenting around you. Though you may be deluded about what you decided to believe, you will defend the integrity of your minds' beliefs to hide your circular reasoning of self-deception. In other words, you believe the world is real because it was made by your belief in it and yet, deny the power of your mind over matter by denying that your mind made the world it experienced. Only in denial can you believe sickness to be real.

The foundation for all addictions to survive is denial. You are in denial about your addiction to the belief in a body-self idea as you defend it as your personal center of being. This belief is the cause of your experience of disease, degeneration, and death, defended as a real life process.

If you realize that all things change there is nothing you will try to hold on to
If you aren't afraid of dying there is nothing you can't achieve

Tao Te Ching #74

The body you seem to have has its pleasures. It also has vulnerabilities, shortcomings, habits and addictions. You prick the skin and it bleeds. To believe you are a body makes all these symptoms look like relevant causes.

However, because these issues are symptoms of a larger cause, to treat them is like treating a heart attack with an aspirin to alleviate the pain. If you are not a body that is just as fleeting as the wind, here one day and gone the next, all these issues of progression become effects of a mistaken mind. What you believe will be your investment. They become non-issues with the changing of your mind. And the paradigm that describes the process of your body as disease, degeneration, regeneration[187] and death is not what you are.

Disease or Process

It may not be difficult to see that your body is a part of Mother Earth process. You may even say that sickness, decay and death of any living organism are the natural process of Mother Earth. Do you think of a flower as suffering disease, degeneration and death when it loses its blossom?[188] Or can you perceive it as part of Mother Earth's majestic circle dance? How you decide to perceive the ever-changing will be your experience (process) to defend your addiction or dispel it.

Is the vehicle you believe to be you a dance through?
Or is it a dirge?
It's up to you ... what dance do you choose[189]

---

[187]Within this paradigm, the concept of spontaneous regeneration (the miracle that suspends this process temporarily) becomes a working dynamic.
[188] *The Way Home p37-39*
[189] *Symbols of Power p165-166*

The pagans would ask "How can the breath of a body be any more sacred than its absence when the earth is completion as the continuity of its cycle?"[190] Mother Earth has no concept of disease. She just does her dance. You have a concept of disease because that is what the effect of a split mind is all about. Being projected and fragmented as confusion, sickness, mental illness and pollution, the denial of your split mind is to be defended at all costs to protect your insanity from detection.

The Cause of all Sickness

By definition, a split mind is a sick mind because it is divided. A divided mind cannot know itself as whole because it is divided about what it is and therefore in conflict about itself. How can a mind, divided about what it is, be aware of an identity beyond its confusion when in confusion it is unaware that it is divided? How can it self-actualize? This is the dilemma of the "unexamined self."

There is something beyond your experience of a split mind ... that is changeless

If you believe healing to be of the body, in the end it will fail you because your body will die. What miracle medicine will heal your body forever? Ponce de León[191] died looking for the "The Fountain of Youth." Is lasting

---

[190] The ethical humanist who has no basis for offense would be offended by this comment. *The Way Home p173-176*

[191] Juan Ponce de León (1460-1521) was a Spanish explorer who spent the last years of his life looking for a legendary spring whose waters had the power to restore youth.

healing inevitable to the mind alone? What does the data suggest?[192]

There is much talk about miracles of spontaneous regeneration. It is plausible to think that mind over matter can heal a body. To an extent, we have all overcome the fear of healing, to affect the body. The placebo effect[193] is the example of using something outside of your mind, a substitute to heal the body because you are too afraid of the power of your mind to heal directly from your mind.[194] This testament to your mind's power to heal also testifies to your mind's ability to deceive itself into thinking health has to do with a body.

Within the context of Mother Earth's dance is the healing of any "body" as a matter of Mother reclaiming her own in the name of "The Cycle of Continuity."[195] How can there be such a thing as disease or sickness when it is all a natural process of what a body does. Even if you contract a sickness because of a manufactured social ill you still end up the same. If you argue, "It depends on how you look at it," you've said everything that's needed to be said. What does the data suggest?

---

[192] *Symbols of Power p22-23*

[193] Little is understood of how the placebo effect works. One theory is that the patient's faith in a cure may be related to the release of brain chemicals called endorphins, the body's natural opiates. Others believe it to be an experience of faith beyond the measurement of brain physiology.

[194] *Symbols of Power p24-25*

[195] *Symbols of Power p43-52*

Summary

To heal the body is temporary
To heal the mind is forever

A mind addicted to the process of a body as its continuity for life would easily mistake *"any deviation from or interruption of the normal structure or function of any body part, organ, or system"* as a threat to its existence. I do not deny that some minutes of time may have been added to your life as a body because a disease was conquered or a medical procedure was successful. However, in the light of the "eternal always" these minutes of quantitative value become meaningless measures of nothingness. Even if there is no "eternal always," what are these minutes to mean? Sounds like an existential dilemma of "being" or a dismissive "so what?"

If your body is not an end in itself, "dust to dust" as a real life process is an irrelevant fiction. NOW your mind is free to use the body as a means for you to recognize passage ... and time becomes your friend. The miracle you wait for on this side of the veil is a fundamental shift in how you perceive what your body is really for. Remember, purpose is meaning. The ever-changing process of mother earth does not witness to birth, decay and death. It witnesses to something else ... your transformation through. Healing is as simple as changing your mind about what you really are. For "You Are" is beyond the process of any concept of disease.

The body is a tool for healing ... when it buys you time to heal your mind

By negating the irrelevant fictions is to allow for what is relevant to be self-revealing. *"What is my bliss and how do I get there?"* Will you reach your bliss through a body that dies? What is true purpose when it comes to your body? What does the data suggest?

J. Technology: The new god

The idea of stability is an illusion. The best you can do with instability is tinker with it. This tinkering is called ... science.

Introduction

> *Kingdoms come and Kingdoms go*
> *And no one can say for sure ... why?*

According to Heraclitus the world is ever-changing and therefore not a place to find stability. Even still, does the earth have something it can teach us?[196]

Environmental philosophy is concerned with issues that arise when human beings interact with the environment. Environmental philosophy asks: "Is an ever-growing worldwide political and economic community in need of a global transformation of thinking for the survival of living organisms and the environment?" Albert Einstein said "We can't solve problems by using the same kind of thinking we used when we created them."

Society at Large in a Constant State of Grief

When we find out that the world does not possess the objective value or meaning that we want it to have or have long since believed it to have, we find ourselves in a crisis.

Nietzsche

---

[196] *Symbols of Power p43-52*

The expression of loss in any relationship is grief. There is a direct correlation that suggests every time you try to identify with something for personal meaning, security and ownership that is not yours to possess, you experience grief. You do not grieve because you lost something that was yours.[197] You grieve because you *tried* to invest in something that was not yours to make you happy.[198] Do the work, work back to the object of your grief; exclude nothing. What does the data suggest?

It is the craftiness of self-deception that says: "I know I am not supposed to possess any one" while you do everything you can to assume connections of dependence. Your motivation to justify this dependence is in your search for meaning, connection, and bliss. Then you experience grief ... over and over again and accept that this is what love is all about by believing a strange idea that love and emotional pain are synonymous. Then you justify the bizarre belief that "Love heals the wound it makes." It is not love that causes pain. It is your idea of love that causes pain. To defend the integrity of a split mind which has none, you make love and fear seem the same. To believe that "to love is to grieve" and then be told that "you do not know what love is because you grieve," would cause you to have a righteous injustice of anger and hurt.

And so, your grief *seems to* witness to the idea that your bliss, once again, slipped through your clenched hands! And so again you search, driven to fill the void of

---

[197] If it was truly yours, you would not have lost it.
[198] I recommend you do not make that comment to someone grieving at a funeral. *The Way Home p180-182*

grief, looking for contentment in something else. Through denial you try to possess, to secure love in a place you find grief over and over again ... in a place it cannot be found. Good luck!

Look around you. Society by and large is in a constant state of grieving. Constantly, the mind of your body seeks to accumulate the security of pleasure while trying to avoid the pain that always comes with the pleasure you seek. Meaningful solutions to your problems are not to be found at the level of interaction between individual bodies.

The Search for that "Something More"

The Search for that "Something More"
It's all been said before

Buddha stated that every living being has the same basic wish; to be happy and to avoid suffering. *Lao-tzu* reflected; release all beliefs and everything falls into place. *Heraclitus* proclaimed; the world is ever-changing and therefore not a place to find stability. *Protagoras* observed; nothing is absolutely good or bad, true or false, and that each individual is therefore his or her own final authority. *Socrates, Plato*, and *Aristotle* challenged the philosophic basis of the sophists, teaching that there is a rational basis for absolute truth and thus morality. *Jesus* said; the Kingdom of God is within you.[199] *Kant* believed

---

[199] Luke 17:20-21 American Standard Version (ASV); The Gospel of Thomas #3. Jesus the Christ (born in Bethlehem in Judea between 8 BC and 4 BC and died around 29 AD) is the central figure of Christianity. Some of the early Jewish

that because we perceive, we cannot know anything directly; that to study reflectively your own mind in process is the process of transcendence. *Hegel* claimed to have worked out a total rational understanding of humanity and history as evolving. *Kierkegaard* stressed the ambiguity and absurdity of the human situation that demands courage for a "Leap of Faith." *Schopenhauer* was convinced that at its core, the universe is not a rational place, that transcendence was necessary. *Nietzsche* argued that a rational will to power will overcome life's absurdity. *Heidegger* argued that human beings can never hope to understand why they are here; instead, each individual must choose a goal and follow it with passionate conviction, aware of the certainty of death and the ultimate meaninglessness of one's life. *Sartre* declared that human beings require a rational basis for their lives but are unable to achieve one, and thus human life is a "futile passion." What are you to believe? And where do you start?

---

followers wanted to see him as the promised deliverer of Israel. Thomas the Apostle understood Jesus teaching that The Kingdom of God was to be an experience within each of us rather than in any person or place outside of you. Paul the Apostle regarded Jesus the "Christ" (anointed one) as God's blood sacrifice, redeemer for all humanity. Some Christians regard Jesus as the incarnate Son of God. The life and teachings of Jesus were matters of confusion to his disciples when Jesus was alive. Dispute over whom or what Jesus was about has continued throughout Christianity's history.

Technology as that "Something More"

For the body's survival, a mutually dependent relationship with mother earth is necessary. Addictions are something else. They are excesses initially driven by the belief you can find happiness in them. Obsessions that occupy your time become its progression. Addictions of all sorts are the forms your progression takes. Gambling, alcohol and drugs, food, sex, cars, relationships, control and power, work, hoarding and money are just a few examples of what can be used to feed your obsessions (dependencies). "For comfort" or "I really need it!" are fancy words of justification that hide your addictions from self-detection. For example, instead of working for natural non-toxic sustainable forms of energy, you chose dependency on oil, gas, and cars. "I have been conditioned to live this way" you justify, or "making changes has its difficulties" or "I need my cell phone to stay connected" you exclaim!

The world we know is living in a hand-me-down shoe
And don't you know that the shoe don't fit
Maybe there's a hole in it
We can't walk so we must sit
While the world goes on and on
Living in a hand–me-down shoe

James Seals
Hand-Me-Down Shoe

I'm not saying big houses, big cars, computers and cell phones are evil. I am saying that these excesses are not "necessities" of life. Rather, *the science that has made*

*survival for the body comfortable has become an addiction
to the mind that is conditioned to depend on it.*

That the earth is an illusion of instability you may still
want to debate. However, exploitation of your body's
relationship with its primary relationship (mother earth)
is not only an example of addiction; your exploitation is
the effect of a mind "out of control." It is a demonstration
of your mind's dis-relation with its self ... projected as a
world. The logic of working to exploit the body's primary
means of survival (mother earth) so the body can have its
comforts must be done through the denial of an out of
control mind looking through the body for its primary
relationship of "something more." Because you are
unaware that your mind's "something more" is not to be
found in a world you projected, you will exploit the body
and the world in your search for "something more" in a
place that isn't.[200]

*To a society whose attitudes have adjusted to the
comforts and complications of an advancing technology,
the teachings of Mother Earth seem incomprehensible.*

Your conditioned addiction is justified as necessary
progress towards the "good life;" that is to make your life
more simple and comfortable. However, and from the
beginning, human beings have spent much time and
energy changing external conditions in their search for
the good life, that "something more." What has been the
result? The insanity of depression, anger, grief, addictions
of all sorts and wars still abound. Your life is not simpler

---

[200] Spiritual dilemma; *Symbols of Power p31-41*

and your stress is an attitude that attacks the comfort of your body. In other words;

The advancement of technology has nothing to do with mental well-being. Technological change is smoke and mirror magic to hide what is really going on.

Gratification beyond Justification

The Cynics[201] *twenty four hundred years ago* contended that civilization, with its attendant ills, was an artificial, unnatural condition and that it should be held in contempt. They advocated returning to a natural life, which they equated with a simple life, maintaining that complete happiness can be attained only through self-sufficiency. Independence is the true good, not riches or luxuries. The Cynics were ascetic believing moderation or abstinence was the key to liberation.

Your conditioning is a crafty seduction on a level more reaching than you realize. As a creature of habit are you continually looking for ways to ingratiate your body? Does economic gain provide you with opportunities to exploit your willingness for self-gratification well beyond any need to secure the comfort of a body? In the name of The Glory of Human Kind are structural icons of steel, concrete and glass, examples of an advancing society? Or do they bear witness to a gratification beyond justification; the new god incognito.[202] How far removed are the minds of this generation from the experience of

---

[201] The Cynics were members of a school of Greek philosophers founded during the second half of the 4th century BC.
[202] In hiding

Mother Earth's teachings? The Cynics have something to teach us. Are you listening?

The god "Technology"[203]

You make amazing technological advances that have amazing technological repercussions. The splitting of the atom for energy has a repercussion of bombs and nuclear waste. Great medical advances are fraught with one ethical dilemma after another. Fertilizers for crop yield that can feed the world are doing what to the food you eat, the soil you deplete and the rivers you pollute? A cell phone that can do just about everything (but beam you up; not yet) when it comes to communicating with anyone who has one, can also be used as a bomb detonator or to connect you with a drug dealer. The mind of human kind is predisposed to project its split as a world of duality, a yin and yang of confusion, mixed messages of conflict. Conflict in philosophy, psychology, theology, politics, economics, and technology has always been the result of the dualistic thinking of a split mind.

Technology, your god of salvation, is a distraction that keeps you from seeing the heart of your real problem. The technocrats tell you that a solution is in the making. They tell you this through the eyes of a conditioned mentality that says technology will solve all of our problems. Technology is economic driven like economics is technologically driven. These two bed partners will attest to the need for each other. This paradigm may be self-validating but it is not revealing. Medicine is always on

---

[203] *Symbols of Power p84*

the brink of a miracle cure ... with a new disease waiting on the horizon to make more waves.

Whether you're ready or not, Mother Earth will make the correction for you. And within the mentality of your denial of what the earth has to teach you,[204] you will pay your dues. Your karma is fueled by the mind that relates to a body until the mind forgives the body it is not.[205]

Summary

The science that has made survival for the body comfortable has become an addiction to the mind that is conditioned to depend on it

When a lake reaches the saturation point of society's runoff, it dies. The pace you now continue has a saturation point. The point is not that technological advances are bad.[206] In itself, technology is not good or bad. However, within human kind's propensity to fool itself over and over again, you have placed on the altar a new god. Your new god; evolving technology is a distraction, smoke screen, magical mirror, your god of human salvation so you can't see where your solution really lies. The evolution of technology has nothing to do with mental well-being. Look again. What does the data scream?

Out of an economic consuming vacuum of dependence, we teach our children "empowerment." And within this

---

[204] *Symbols of Power p48*
[205] *Symbols of Power p98-105*
[206] *Symbols of Power P45-46;* under the section "Progress"

paradigm of educational conditioning are the tools they use. How can you ask anyone to reach beyond what they have been taught to depend on? Beyond the teaching of the world, clear of the illusion of cultural conditioning is an understanding of what "empowerment" means.

The data suggests that there is a complication of information that makes it difficult to see the nothingness of its contradiction.

J. The Scientist's Dilemma

Nietzsche asserted that the scientific assumption of an orderly universe is for the most part ... a useful fiction

A Brief History of Epistemology

Epistemology (Greek episteme, "knowledge"; logos, "theory") is a branch of philosophy that addresses the philosophical problems surrounding the theory of knowledge.

In the 5th century BC, the Greek Sophists questioned the possibility of reliable and objective knowledge. A leading sophist, *Gorgias,* argued that nothing really exists, that if anything did exist it could not be known, and that if knowledge were possible, it could not be communicated. Another prominent sophist, *Protagoras,* maintained that no person's opinions can be said to be more correct than another's, because each is the sole judge of his or her own experience.

Plato, following his teacher *Socrates,* tried to answer the Sophists by postulating the existence of a world of unchanging and invisible forms, or ideas, about which it is possible to have exact and certain knowledge. *Aristotle* followed Plato in regarding abstract knowledge as superior to any other, but disagreed with him as to the proper method of achieving it. Aristotle maintained that almost all knowledge is derived from experience.

Before the time of Thomas Aquinas, Western thought had been dominated by the philosophy of *Saint Augustine,*[207]

---

[207] Saint Augustine (354-430) is considered the greatest of the Latin Fathers and one of the most eminent theologians of the

the Western church's great Father of the 4th and 5th centuries, who taught that in the search for truth people must depend upon sense experience. *Saint Thomas Aquinas[208]* followed Aristotle in regarding perception as the starting point and logic as the intellectual procedure for arriving at reliable knowledge of nature, but he considered faith in scriptural authority as the main source of religious belief.

From the 17th to the late 19th century, the main issue in epistemology was reasoning vs. sense perception in acquiring knowledge. For the rationalists, of whom the French philosopher *René Descartes,* the Dutch philosopher *Baruch Spinoza,* and the German philosopher *Gottfried Wilhelm Leibniz[209]* were the leaders, the main source and final test of knowledge was deductive reasoning[210] based on self-evident principles. For the empiricists, beginning with the English philosophers

---

Roman Catholic Church.

[208] Saint Thomas Aquinas (1225-1274) was an Italian philosopher and theologian, whose works have made him the most important figure in Scholastic philosophy and one of the leading Roman Catholic theologians.

[209] Gottfried Wilhelm Leibniz (1646-1716) was a German philosopher, mathematician, and statesman, regarded as one of the supreme intellects of the 17th century.

[210] Deductive reasoning is the process of reasoning from one or more general statements (premises) to reach a logically certain conclusion. For example; if all men are mortal and Socrates is a man, then Socrates is mortal. The premise is false if the conclusion is invalid. The scientific method uses deduction to test hypotheses and theories.

Francis Bacon[211] and *John Locke*, the main source and final test of knowledge was sense perception.

Bacon introduced the new era of modern science by criticizing the medieval reliance on tradition and authority and also by setting down new rules of a scientific method, including the first set of rules of inductive logic.[212] Locke attacked the rationalist belief that the principles of knowledge are intuitively self-evident, arguing that all knowledge is derived from experience, either from experience of the external world, which stamps sensations on the mind, or from internal experience, in which the mind reflects on its own activities. Locke claimed that human knowledge of external physical objects is always subject to the errors of the senses, and he concluded that one cannot have absolute certain knowledge of the physical world.

The German philosopher *Immanuel Kant* attempted a compromise between empiricism and rationalism,

---

[211] Francis Bacon (1561-1626) was an English philosopher and statesman, one of the pioneers of modern scientific thought. He maintained that all prejudices and preconceived attitudes, which he called idols, must be abandoned. He was an important influence on the development of empiricism.

[212] Inductive reasoning, the opposite of deductive reasoning, makes broad generalizations from specific observations. For example, "A large enough asteroid impact would create a very large crater and cause a severe impact winter that could drive the non-avian dinosaurs to extinction. We observe that there is a very large crater in the Gulf of Mexico dating to very near the time of the extinction of the non-avian dinosaurs. Therefore it is possible that this impact could explain why the non-avian dinosaurs went extinct."

restricting knowledge to the domain of experience, and thus agreeing with the empiricists, but attributing to the mind a function in incorporating sensations into the structure of experience. This structure could be known *"a priori"* or innately without resorting to empirical methods, and in this respect Kant agreed with the rationalists. To Kant, to study reflectively, your own mind in process, is the process of transcendence.

Not unlike the Greek Sophist philosophers 24 centuries before him, *Edmund Husserl*[213] took Kant's thoughts on "things in themselves" and *our experience* of "things in themselves" asserting that we cannot know anything directly because our experience of any object is different than the object itself. This makes the study of any object (the objective thing in itself) irrelevant and the study or reflection of our experience of any object (the subjective), everything.

Albert Einstein stated that; a man "experiences himself, his thoughts and feelings as something separate from the rest; a kind of optical delusion of his consciousness. This delusion is a kind of prison for us, restricting us to our personal desires. Not to nourish the delusion but to try to overcome it is the way to reach the attainable measure of peace of mind."

To simplify an understanding of the preceding babble taken from the mouths of the great intellectual wisdom

---

[213]Husserl introduced the term "phenomenological reduction" for his method of reflection on the meanings the mind employs when it contemplates an object. Because this method concentrates on meanings that are in the mind, whether or not the object contemplated actually exists is irrelevant. Husserl greatly influenced Heidegger and Sartre.

seekers of times gone by, it would be hard to know what to believe about how you know what you know. If John Locke is correct that human knowledge of external physical objects is always subject to the errors of the senses and therefore one cannot have absolute certain knowledge of the physical world, your search for meaning through the world leads you to where? If Husserl and the Sophists are correct in saying that it's not what you observe that has meaning, it's your interpretation of what you observe that has meaning; that beauty actually does belong to the eye of each beholder in all things; your search for meaning in the world leads you to where? If Einstein is correct, that you are an optical delusion of consciousness, a prisoner of your own desire, your search for meaning leads you to where?

Because it is the nature of perception or "to perceive" that brings your mind into the arena of uncertainty, what does an ever-changing world of instability as you perceive it have to teach you? The data suggests that complicating the results of information makes it difficult to see its nothingness.

Observer as Participant

There is no such thing as "objectivity" for the scientist

That movement and noise happens is a given just as "things in themselves" are what they are. What meaning these things may have is a disposition of subjecting yourself to your object of study. Because the idea of meaning always makes the observer a participant, studying anything apart from your interaction with it is not possible. In the ephemeral, whether it is interpreted as order or chaos, everything is in relation to you or is in dis-relation to you, *as you choose to see it*. Because this is so, no conclusion can be definitive in the realm of experimentation, study, and testing until all factors are considered. Inductively[214] speaking, not all factors can be considered when it comes to a universe of interconnected relationships. But generalizations can be inferred.[215]

Deductively speaking;

1) Hypothesis: All observers participate within a context that involves relationship. There is no other context outside of this relationship.

2) All objects of study have meaning personal to each individual within that context. In other words, you are always a part of what you apprehend or grasp mentally.

3) Therefore, the idea of an objective world or a world outside of your mind is an illusion.[216]

To observe is to participate. Therefore, to make a preliminary assumption (hypothesis) out of interest is to qualify for meaning. This assessment for meaning is a "leap of faith" that assumes an outcome of usefulness (value). Within the context of the ephemeral the meanings all relationships have are subject to a perception of uncertainty. Society is a collective hunch of

---

[214] Discretely or one at a time

[215] To infer is to conclude from evidence or a premise. "Socrates argued that a statue inferred the existence of a sculptor." (Plato's Academy) Theists and Deists erroneously argue that an orderly universe infers a supreme creator.

[216] *The Way Home p113*

negotiated perceptions. The meanings you have made out of your relationships (personal or impersonal), are up to you unless ... *reality is not yours to select.* How many times do you have to see that how you perceive other people is habitually not accurate and counter intuitive to your peace of mind? That you selectively perceive instances that tell you your gut feelings have been right about someone is just that, selective in the light of all the times you have been wrong!

To Kant, to study reflectively your own mind in process is the process of transcendence. To Carl Jung, "To look outside is to dream, to look inside is to wake up." These are statements that transcend Sophist ideology.

The Scientific Method[217]

The only empirical truth is that nothing is ever the same[218]

1) To measure is to qualify. This assumes that quantitative amounts of data mean something.

2) To make data mean something is to make it personal. It is taking the objective and making it subjective. It is "a leap of faith" to make the quantitative qualitative.

---

[217] The Scientific Method is a systematic approach to research. It is an ideology based on the philosophy of the empiricist approach. It is standardized rules for the collecting and processing raw data, quantified through numbers (statistics) and qualified as meaningful through "a leap of faith" called the interpretation of test results.

[218] Einstein was a proponent of the uncertainty principle, which states that precision in measuring processes is limited.

3) No matter how you gather or organize the data, the source of the data is always ever-changing.

4) Therefore, the data always says one of two things;

Either it's all metaphor for your journey or
Eat, drink and be merry for tomorrow you will die!

Because all relationships are in flux, to measure is to approximate. If the Scientific Method of data collection and correlations of outcomes is *assumed* to be "the reliable approach" for meaning, scientific consensus for standardized testing becomes essential for the exchange of mutual communication and understanding. Symbols are defined and empowered according to their purpose of practical application. And because the observer cannot be impartial to his study of interest, paradigms become established assumptions to your object of study. Can meaning be found here?

I read the news today ... oh boy
Four thousand holes in Blackburn Lancashire
And though the holes were rather small
They had to count them all
Now they know how many holes it takes to fill the Albert Hall
I'd love to turn you on

Lennon & McCartney
A Day in the Life

Validity[219] and reliability[220] factors set the parameters for your paradigm while your paradigm justifies the need for validity and reliability factors. As long as your data falls within the measures your paradigm demands, the data collected will testify to the truth of your results, always within the limits of your paradigm. If I propose (hypothesis) that evil is the killing of another, then whoever kills another demonstrates that evil is real. And you know that evil is real because someone was killed. This is an example of circular reasoning that is not revealing.

There is "no exit" from this self-deception unless you recognize any threat for what it really is: an exception to the validity of your ideology.[221] How can you evaluate a belief system's validity when you use the rules of those beliefs to justify the validity of that system? Beauty belongs to the eye of the beholder. Ugliness belongs to the eye of the beholder. Because you see something in a way that makes you angry is to you justified anger, not because your anger is justified but because you see it that

[219] Validity is the extent to which a test measures what it claims to measure. Do IQ tests measure intelligence?

[220] A measure is said to have a high reliability if it produces similar results under consistent conditions. However, in the ever-changing the lack of consistent conditions limits a test's usefulness. Also, because culture biases regarding IQ testing, not only is reliability limited but its validity for measuring what it says it measures is low.

[221] An ideology is a set of beliefs, values, and opinions that shapes the way a person or a group such as a social class thinks, acts, and understands the world.

way. For every proof you have that evil is real, I can show you ignorance.

You perceive what you project and deny your projection. If projection makes perception, what you perceive is always true to you not because it is true but because your mind will only select to perceive that which will validate what you already believe. Your beliefs are always self-validating because you already believe them. That does not make them self-revealing unless you are aware of your reflection rather than experiencing your projection as out there. And to reflect rather than project is to admit without exception that there is no world outside of your mind. What you think is "out there" is a projection unknown to you because it was made out of the conflict of a split mind.

A good traveler has no fixed plans and is not intent on arriving
A good artist lets his intuition lead him wherever it wants
A good scientist has freed himself of concepts and keeps his mind open to what is

Tao Te Ching #27

Your accumulation of data in the manifestation[222] of the ever-changing can only have an ever-changing

---

[222] Just as a cloud is considered real to the body's senses, so are all manifestations of nature considered real to the body's senses; just as the body's senses are a manifestation of nature. Yet, because these manifestations of nature are ever-changing appearances, they are deceiving because they are appearances. Everything the mind beholds through the body's senses are

conclusion. Empirically speaking, the ever accumulating of data testifies to that fact. Awareness is the outcome of reflection, looking outside of the paradigm altogether. Your ideology of the scientific method of study will not allow you to think divergently on this matter. The smoke and mirror of an ever-changing nothingness does not have a meaningful teleology.[223] Complicating the results of information makes it difficult to see its nothingness. This is what the data suggests.

Scientific Evolution, Teleology & Being

Evolution is an illusion of conditioned thinking
To see progress in an ever-changing spin is self-deception

Though they would deny it, religious apologists[224] fell into the trap of explaining "God" as unchangeably eternal yet the maker of a material world of change. As God's creation as physical bodies, we would be part of the world of God's creation. *Process Thought*[225] took it one

---

effects; everything. To not recognize these manifestations as temporary in nature is to cultivate attachments. These manifestations of "effect" as attachments become your means to pleasure and pain, happiness and sadness. To quantify (number, compare, contrast) manifestations as meaningful is the empiricist's dilemma of making meaningful ever-changing manifestations. And though you are not the product of nature vs. nature, you do play out your sickness (spiritual dilemma) through the guise (manifestations) of nature and nurture.

[223] Outcome

[224] Defenders of the faith

[225] Or Process Theology is a type of theology developed from Alfred North Whitehead (1861–1947). Whitehead

step further saying if God made the world and is in a relationship with his creation, then He is in some way part of the world's progression. The apologists fall into a battle against the evolutionists with unbelievably irrational confusion by defending the idea that God had something to do with the creation of an ever-changing material world[226] while trying to deny or modify an evolution of change.

Simply speaking, if "Being" is not based on the ephemeral, then you are not a body of change but something else. Therefore, the physical realm of "The Evolution of the Species"[227] as cause and effect becomes irrelevant for conversation because it has nothing to do with what you are as "Being." This also makes the idea of scientific evolution (the earth sciences) irrelevant to *Ontology.*[228] If you choose a concept of non-being, or being a part of the physical realm of earth cycles, the idea

believed it to be an essential attribute of God to affect and be affected by temporal processes. Because God interacts with the changing universe, God is changeable (that is to say, God is affected by the actions that take place in the universe) over the course of time. However, the abstract elements of God (goodness, wisdom, etc.) remain eternally.

[226] *The Way Home p128*

[227] Charles Robert Darwin (1809-1882) was a British scientist who laid the foundation of modern evolutionary theory with his concept of the development of all forms of life through the slow-working process of natural selection. His work was of major influence on the life and earth sciences and on modern thought in general.

[228] Ontology as the most general branch of metaphysics is the study of "being." Because it is a field of study, it is once removed from experiencing "Being" directly.

of scientific evolution remains irrelevant. There is no teleology[229] (aim, end, goal, purpose) in non-being except for how you would like your funeral to be played out. It is the atheistic existentialists' view that the concept of non-being makes today's choice irrelevant to purpose or meaning.

Cosmology's Big Bang[230]

The Tao can't be perceived
Smaller than an electron
It contains uncountable galaxies

Tao Te Ching #32

---

[229] Teleology (Greek telos, "end"; logos, "discourse") in philosophy is the science or doctrine that attempts to explain the universe in terms of ends or final causes. Teleology is based on the proposition that the universe has design and purpose. In Christian theology, teleology represents a basic argument for the existence of God, in that the order and efficiency of the natural world seem not to be accidental. If the world design is intelligent, an ultimate Designer must exist. *Hmm, is how the world operates a design that reflects intelligence?* Teleologists oppose interpretations of the universe that rely solely on organic development or natural causation. The impact of Charles Darwin's theories of evolution, which hold that species develop by natural selection, has greatly reduced the influence of traditional teleological arguments. Yet, I find Darwin's theory of "natural selection" to be teleologically progressive in purpose.

[230] Cosmology is the study of the physical nature and form of the universe as a whole. Physics is a science within this whole.

Theorists speculate that the universe started from energy smaller than an atom and in an instant exploded into a *projection* of energy evolving as matter and is still evolving. Was there a thought behind this *dividing projection of energy*[231] smaller than an atom?

The Big Bang, as an instant of conscious thought was divided and subdivided so what is the same could look like seemingly endless parts. Time and space as an effect of this Big Bang becomes a place to put all these seemingly endless different parts and people to function in. It is the dollhouse in the living room that hides the fact that all these people are functioning in a make believe fiction.

The Big Bang was not an explosion in space to experience time; it is an explosion of space in your minds' past. In the light of this, what is relevant to debate about?

Lost in the Stars

It is often nobly stated that we can find out about our origins by gazing out at the stars. You may have a vague *intuition* of a reality beyond your ephemeral experience. This intuition, "beyond your ephemeral experience" is not a place in the stars. Meaning or purpose will not be found far away behind the romanticizing of a shiny star. It is in you. That faraway place is another form of the projection of your split mind, an ever-changing smoke and mirror calling you across the universe.

---

[231] *Symbols of Power p32*

Sounds of laughter shades of earth are ringing through my open views ... Inciting and inviting me
Limitless undying love which shines around me like a million suns ... It calls me on and on ...
Across the universe

Lennon & McCartney
Across The Universe

To project a split mind would be to experience this split as an inner and outer world. Your outer world experience projected as if external to your mind is what you communicate through as metaphors. Useful as your metaphors[232] may be in your attempt to want to express and know, they are your inner experiences projected and conceptualized as a cosmological orientation.

How did I find myself so far away?
I must be living in the stars
I didn't know how far I'd fallen astray
Away from your loving arms
But I remember you once told me
True love never dies
Here I am ...
Lost in the stars of your sky

Matt Karayan
Lost In the Stars

---

[232] Aesthetics as one of the main branches of philosophy is the study of the nature of beauty in the fine arts.

The metaphors of your projection that you colorfully and cleverly examine, describe, flirt with, explain, grapple with, and fight for, are your attempts to find out what you forgot. You forget that you already know. An ah-ha experience is a momentary remembrance of what you already know. You will not find your answer in the stars. There seems to be a power in the universe. But it belongs to you, projected as a lost and confused star. Stop looking for meaning in the world of your projection. It is but an effect of a confused mind, lost in the stars of its sky.

What makes one a great teacher?
The one who lives within
What makes one able to contemplate the universe
through a dewdrop?
The one who knows one thing more than everybody else
What is that one more thing to know?
To know you know nothing ... and can therefore rest
in the way things are
That's what makes one a great teacher

Space & Time[233]

According to Emmanuel Kant, *objects in and of themselves have no existence, and space and time exist only as part of the mind, as "intuitions" by which perceptions are measured and judged.* Your dualistic mind is a split point of view, a reference point of comparison, needed to communicate understanding about your "intuitions" ... as space and time.

---

[233] *Symbols of Power p60-61*

We join spokes together in a wheel
But it is the center hole that makes the wagon move
We shape clay into a pot
But it is the emptiness inside that holds whatever we
want
We hammer wood for a house
But it is the inner space that makes it livable
We work with being
But non-being is what we use

Tao Te Ching #11

Between objects of distance is measurement called space. In other words, distance implies a relationship of space between objects. Time is the measure of movement. The clock ticks the earth spins and a twenty-four-hour spin is measured as a day. The earth spins as it rotates into a four-season cycle. A four-season cycle as it revolves around the sun is an earth year. Your age is the measure of how many times your body has been around the sun. All movement of objects is between space and time's reference point. All of this is a continuous adjustment of approximations. There are times that you have to adjust your watch because all relationships of motion are not consistently exact or because your battery ran low. What's the difference?

Because everything is always moving, there is no stationary point of reference. Earth is like a ship sailing in an ocean of space. Polaris, the current North Star,[234]

---

[234] North Star, our current Polestar, is located closest to the point toward which the axis of the earth is directed, thus roughly marking the location of the north celestial pole. The

considered a stable point of reference, is another ship sailing in the same ocean. Between objects is space, the void of nothingness. What is beyond the movement of objects? "Projecting our images in space and in time" infers a "place" (center) from which to project. Is there such a place that makes "out there" irrelevant?

As regards to time and simply stated, the only place guilt can survive is in the memory of your mind. Though time is not real, your temptation to make the past as meaningful memories in the present, allows your mind time and space for the entertainment of guilt. And, the idea of paying for the past in the future makes the present a transition from the past to the future. Your hope for a better future out of a guilty past robs you of the experience of the present. What happened to the present, the only tense there is? Time is not real; it is a figment of your imagination. Your mind's experience of a past and future tense that is not real clearly demonstrates the fact of what an illusion is; it is your constant experience of tenses that are not real

Tomorrow is the yesterday that is happening today

---

positions of the celestial poles change as the earth's axis moves. Different stars become the North Star. During the past 5000 years the line of direction of the North Pole has moved from the star Thuban to within one degree of the bright star Polaris in the constellation Ursa Minor (Little Dipper), which is now the North Star. In the year 7500, the brightest star in the constellation Cepheus, Alpha (a) Cephei, will mark the pole, and in the year 15,000 the star Vega, in the constellation Lyra, will be the North Star. About 9000 years after that, Polaris will again become the North Star. What a wobble!

Summary

How you collect random data may be standardized. However, it's not unusual for scientists to have different views of the data. What does that tell you?

1) A mind split does not know itself (the making of the unconscious) and will therefore experience intrapersonal opposition.

2) The split of intrapersonal opposition is unconsciously projected as a world outside of your mind as a way of trying to get rid of the opposition of your internal conflict.

3) The unconscious projection is the making of an inner and outer world; the interpersonal; the realm of consciousness; the duality of subject and object.

4) Duality as comparison, differences, measuring and opposition is your conscious way of trying to understand the unconscious projection of your inner and outer world.

Perceiving comparisons, degrees, and levels is the example of an uncertain mind. Your continued focus on measuring degrees of ever-changing uncertainty for meaning is the means for continued evolving uncertainty. There is nothing wrong with the scientific method of collecting data for meaning. But does it measure anything of relevance? The scientific method is not justified in its presumption that "it collects data to generate information that is helping us evolve."

Your desire to validate your experiences as something real is your attempt to make your projected confusion a meaningful experience. To measure is one of your attempts to make your projected confusion a meaningful experience.

Nietzsche asserted that the scientific assumption of an orderly universe is for the most part ... a useful fiction. At one time, and understandably, the scientific method was a breath of fresh air from the ideology of religious authority as being definitive truth. Now your mind needs to be freed from the ideological religion of the scientific method.

To negate the scientific method as a reliable way to attain knowledge would leave you with what? To negate the scientific method as a reliable way to attain meaningful information about the world would leave you with what? To negate the scientific assumption of an orderly universe would leave you with what? What does the data suggest? That reality is not yours to select.

To some, knowledge is derived as your experience of "being" through your unreliable perception of an uncertain world. To Kant, knowledge could be derived from your experience of an outer world and inner world. To others, knowledge is your experience of "being," other than your perceptions of the world.

Because perception is not an attribute of your Source of Being, your experience of transcendence[235] is your journey home. The only function that perception could have would be to lead you beyond it to knowledge. And this would be a temporary function.

---

[235] *The Way Home p192*

K. The Existentialist's Dilemma

He's a real Nowhere Man
Sitting in his Nowhere Land
Making all his Nowhere Plans
For Nobody

Lennon & McCartney
Nowhere Man

No Exist

Last thing I remember – I was running for the door
I had to find the passage back to the place I was before
"Good night," said the night man, "we are programmed
to receive"
"You can check out any time you like – but you can never
leave"

The Eagles
Hotel California

When the *practically minded* existentialist[236] looked out to observe the world, what he found was random

---

[236]Kierkegaard, Nietzsche, and other existential writers have been deliberately unsystematic in the exposition of their philosophies, preferring to express themselves in aphorisms, dialogues, parables, and other literary forms. Despite their anti-rationalist position, most existentialists cannot be said to be irrationalists in the sense of denying all validity to rational thought. They have held that rational clarity is desirable

exceptions to any definitive empirical conclusion.[237] "As it
appears" stated the existentialist, "the only constant
principle of truth is that everything observable is ever-
changing. There is nothing to hang my hat on but to ask
'To be, or not to be, that is the question?'"[238]

The existential *atheist* has a point when he steps from
quantitative data to a qualitative "leap of faith" by
concluding,

> *Unless God is psycho*
> *There is no God in this world*
> *How could there be?*
> *This world is absurd![239]*

"To authenticate my existence" states the *ethical*
existential *humanist*,[240] "I can make a moral decision by

---

wherever possible, but that the most important questions in
life are not accessible to reason or science. Furthermore, they
have argued that science is not as rational as is commonly
supposed. Nietzsche asserted that the scientific assumption of
an orderly universe is for the most part a useful fiction.
[237] There is no such thing as a "definitive empirical conclusion"
unless you consider the phrase "The only thing absolute is
change."
[238] The opening phrase of a soliloquy in the "Nunnery
Scene" of William Shakespeare's play *Hamlet*
[239] *The Way Home* p66-67
[240]Generally, humanism refers to a perspective that affirms
some vague notion of "human value." In modern times,
humanist movements are typically aligned with secularism and
non-theistic religions.

183

doing the right thing on behalf of humanity." The right thing for purpose and meaning in the absurdity of the ever-changing for the humanistic existential atheist is "a leap of faith" to believe there is something that can come out of the absurdity of the meaningless. Even though there is "no exit,"[241] the humanistic existential atheist seems to be sure about one thing; "life means what you want it to mean." If that is the case, why should a humanistic creed be more sacred than anything else?

Doesn't have a point of view
Knows not where he's going to
Isn't he a bit like you and me

Lennon & McCartney
Nowhere Man

Situational ethics reigns for the atheistic existential humanist for "To be or not to be" is the only absolute act in the name of the *individual* for humanity. The interpretation of movement and noise as a collective hunch is what he calls "Society." Yet, no matter how he leaps for an "absolute sacred doctrine," he can find "no exit" from the absurdity of his projection he calls a world of paradoxically random events. In other words, the existential atheist cannot afford to look at their foundational reason for being an altruistic human being, because there is none.

---

[241]Sartre; His one act play, *Huis Closor* or *No Exit*, first produced in Paris in May, 1944, is the clearest example and metaphor for his philosophy.

The atheistic existentialist may be right about the absurdity of a world that no god in his or her right mind could have allowed. The thing that the existential atheist missed is; because he perceives the world as absurd, he allows no room for an experience of "Being" that transcends his decision that *only perceives* that all there is, is the absurd. Self-deception is deciding what is real and then selecting only those samples that prove your point. However, beyond your selective samples of random events for meaning is an experience of being other than the sum of its parts that you can't know intellectually.[242]

In what ways do you violate your mind about "what is" by adding what is not there to make the absurd a meaningfully authentic experience?[243] Constantly you react to your fearful or angry interpretations of what is not there. And by some magical "leap of faith" you circumnavigate the "no exit" sign with distractions of ritualistic behaviors, rites of passage, sacred writings of belief and meaningless empirical data to try to understand the room of the absurd, as a way to avoid your inevitable fate in the "no exist" of death. Yes, life as

---

[242] Thought does precede its own experience and "Being" precedes thought. Descartes' built his whole philosophy on the premise that thought precedes "Being" as the proof for the existence of God. However, this is merely a demonstration that God was created out of our own thinking (anthropomorphism). Because denial precedes projection, we have many gods created out of the projection of our thoughts. Those who are mad at God are mad at a god they made. Either reality is yours to select or *"Being already Is"* ... beyond thought.

[243] Not only are we talking about selective perception but also of a denial that breeds delusion.

you perceive it is a circus; at best a comedy of errors. The question is not "Is there life after death?" The question is, "Is there death?"[244] And if death of a body is an irrelevant concept, what does all of this really mean?[245]

The existential *empiricist* may claim no icon. But *Process Thought*[246] based on selective perception becomes their god. Any attempt to hang value on movement and noise is the religious dilemma of making icons of faith out of the process of "ashes to ashes and dust to dust."

Religion is not the only "opium of the masses."[247] An exit from the absurd paradoxes the world offers by

---

[244] *The Way Home p172*
[245] *Symbols of Power p31-42*
[246] Process Philosophy like Process Theology is a speculative world-view, which asserts that *basic reality* is constantly in a process of flux and change. Reality is identified with pure process. Concepts such as creativity, freedom, novelty, emergence, and growth are fundamental explanatory categories for process philosophy. This metaphysical perspective is to be contrasted with a philosophy of substance; the view that a fixed and permanent reality underlies the changing or fluctuating world of ordinary experience (Plato). Whereas substance philosophy emphasizes static being, process philosophy emphasizes dynamic becoming. Process philosophy is as old as the 6th century BC Greek philosopher Heraclitus and then renewed by Hegel. Interest in process thought was stimulated in the 19th century by the theory of evolution.
[247] The full quote from Karl Marx translates as: "Religion is the sigh of the oppressed creature, the heart of a heartless world, and the soul of soulless conditions. It is the opium of the people."

looking at a world of contradictions and drama for solutions and meaning has always been sought through the religion of the day. It has been cloaked in differing undetectable forms. Our current religious saviors, to name a few, are our ever-changing educational curriculums' and science technology. However, there is an experience of knowing that is not an exit as much as it is an awareness that transcends a world of meaningless evolving fictions. Complicating the results of information does make it difficult to see its nothingness.

Beyond the self-deception of selective perception is a mindful view, open enough to look ... to look through the "no exist" curtain of the ephemeral.

The Concept of Ego

I define ego as *a constellation of selective self-validating fictions strung together*[248] as a way to make sense out of what can never make sense. The ego mind, as a way to explain your world is actually a block to understanding anything. Fear is the result of not knowing while to not know is to perceive. Your attempt to make sense out of the absurd to avoid fear is actually the cause of your fear. For example, if you believe evil is real (a fearful concept), out of fear you will want to understand it to deal with it or avoid it. However, because you already decided that evil is real, you will see events in the world that demonstrate evil. No matter how hard you try to deal with evil through magical beliefs and rituals of prayer for

---

[248] How loose and how tight these false beliefs are strung together are the psychological basis for neurosis, psychosis and your potential for awareness.

protection, you can't get rid of it. Why? Because the concept of evil was made real by you in your mind. Therefore, wherever you go to protect yourself from evil, you take it with you. No matter how deep your moat is and how strong your doors are and how fortified your walls are, you are the one who brought evil into your castle of safety. And so it is for you to live fearfully inside of your walls of safety. And no matter how hard you try to get rid of it with magical thinking and rituals of faith, evil is not out there!

As a child you don't open the closet door for fear of what might be in there. And so it is, you live in fear anyway ... of what might be behind the door of the unknown, inside your castle walls. Your experience of evil as real does not make it real. Your investment in the belief that evil is real is what makes it real to you alone with other ego alliances.

It is you who depreciates the power your mind has to move mountains.[249] Perception always brings your mind into the arena of uncertainty. That is why your search for truth through all that the world has to offer makes you a frustrated learner. And because the world was made so you could never find truth, your search to nowhere continues from nowhere.[250]

---

[249] That you have done this to yourself is just below your conscious level and is the basis for all guilt and fear; guilt for the violation of depreciating the power you are and through the eyes of guilt, fear of punishment from the power you are. That is the reason you fear healing through the power of your mind and need the substitutions of placebos. That is also the reason you are your own worst enemy. The Gospel of Thomas #106, Matthew 17:20, 21:21, Mark 11:23

Nowhere Man ... please listen
You don't know ... what you're missing
Nowhere Man ... The world is at your command

Lennon & McCartney
Nowhere Man

There is a direct correlation between following the dictates of the ego and being a frustrated learner. You are a frustrated learner because the ego sends you on a journey to seek for a solution in the details of a place where none can be found. The world can be considered as the ego's kingdom of dust to dust for meaning and purpose ... before you die. Your epicurean[251] search to find pleasure and avoid pain is a further distraction along your journey to occupy your time. The world is not a place to find meaningful answers because it is constantly being made by "ego you" so you don't find the exit ... as you stumble over the clutter of a room you arranged to get lost in.

---

[250] *The Way Home p179*

[251] Epicureanism is a system of philosophy based chiefly on the teachings of the Greek philosopher Epicurus (341-270 BC). The essential doctrine of Epicureanism is that pleasure is the supreme good and main goal of life. Intellectual pleasures are preferred to sensual ones, which tend to disturb peace of mind. True happiness, Epicurus taught, is the serenity resulting from the conquest of fear of the gods, of death, and of the afterlife. The ultimate aim of all Epicurean speculation about nature is to rid people of such fears.

Failed Relationships

He's as blind as he can be
Just sees what he wants to see
Nowhere Man can you see me at all

Lennon & McCartney
Nowhere Man

To be lost in what appears to be a failed relationship is to suffer. The ego offers many possibilities as to what went wrong. And within these possibilities are innumerable opportunities to justify your experience of guilt, failure, anger, retribution and fear. Maybe someone cheated? Maybe drugs were involved to mess things up? Maybe one became disinterested in the relationship for whatever reason? Beyond any reason you may devise as to why the relationship failed is the principle of a larger picture. From the view of a larger picture, the reason becomes irrelevant. This is because a view *from outside* of the analysis of selected reasons allows for a view of the situation that is not conflictual. As Einstein said;

We *can't solve problems by using the same kind of thinking we used when we created them.*

For example, from the ego's view retribution for what was done to you can easily be justified. The ego says you were abandoned. But if you were to introduce a reframing that is non-dualistic by saying *"It's not that my relationship did not work as much as it is that I gave it the wrong goals,"* you would lend your mind the ability to transcend your belief in abandonment. You give your mind room to view your so-called failed relationship from a different point of view.[252] When you understand that you came together for a reason other than what you decided your relationship "should" have been, you are free from personalizing blame and guilt. There is a larger purpose than you realized, larger than "your little design" you put on the relationship. You bring the problem back to the place it was made, in your thinking. This approach is not about justifying anyone's behavior. It's about you giving your mind room to say, "Oh, I never thought about it that way." An epiphany towards your awakening is a glimpse, collapse in time, speedup, which lies beyond your tools that made the problem real to you.

When you generalize this lesson to all relationships, time collapses[253] for you in a way you never imagined. Furthermore, this one simple example is a resolution that lends itself towards a unified mind.[254] It is one step towards a unified goal by undoing dualistic thinking. You are not trying to justify any behaviors or attitudes, but you are learning to recognize and internalize a principle that says *"Everyone seeks happiness but most of us do not know how to go about getting there."*[255] This view reframes *all* the issues of morality and evil. A unified goal for *peace of mind* will free you to look through your ideology of how you think the world "should" work.

---

[252] The therapeutic art of reframing; *Symbols of Power p23-24*
[253] Less lessons to learn means there is less time needed for you to awaken; thus time collapses. *Symbols of Power p201, 95*
[254] *Symbols of Power p22*
[255] Socrates believed people were not willfully bad, just self-defeating out of ignorance. Jesus thought the same. Luke 23:34

Lasting solutions to the problems in relationships will not be found at the level of interaction between bodies. Resolution between bodies as interactions is to be understood within a larger context. Generalize this principle to all your affairs that the world seems to present and the world disappears.

The Whole

There is *an experience* beyond words, understood as "the Whole." But *it is only experienced as other than* the sum of its parts.[256] The whole is *experienced only as known* rather than analyzed in parts to be added up for meaning. To the empirical scientist of sensation and perception this experience does not make sense ... until it is experienced beyond the selection of sensation and perception. Also, unlike Process Philosophy or the Hegelian philosophy of the synthesis of opposites for a resolution to a higher truth, the whole is not an evolving intellectually rational process rising to a better understanding of the world. From the view of the whole, the ever-changing flux and flow of Heraclitus and Hegel's paradigm towards synthesis is to be transcended all together.

---

[256] According to Gestalt psychology, images are perceived as a pattern or a whole rather than merely as a sum of distinct component parts. The parts derive their nature and purpose from the whole and cannot be understood apart from it. Moreover, a straightforward summation process of individual elements cannot account for the whole. That is why the whole is "other" than rather than "greater" than the sum of its parts.

Questions & Comments

Heraclitus suggests that if the transitory is unstable and that stability is an illusion, why would you invest there? Why would you build your house on a flood plain that floods or on a hill-side that slides except in denial? Is your investment in the unstable a witness to you not understanding what it is you think you are looking at? Is there a direct correlation to trying to make the meaningless mean something that justifies reactions of anger, guilt, depression, anxiety, frustration, loss and fear? If so, how can you advocate on behalf of your own best interests when you don't know that you don't know what your best interests are?[257] Can you come to an understanding of what you are from the instability of the transitory? If you can't know "you" from your reflection of what the world seems to offer, you can't but "see the world wrong and then say it deceives you."[258] Your search for self-esteem through an ever-changing illusive cluster of beliefs is what makes you a frustrated learner. Your lessons in teaching yourself you are worthwhile through your accomplishments in the world is a ruse to ingratiate the ego. "You Are" other than anything you think the world says you are. The concept of "positive thinking" is a delay to try to make the world meaningful; more smoke and mirrors. Your denial of your faulty thought process results in you reacting to something that isn't. Daily you react to your *misinterpretation* of some person and event and don't know that you do it. What it means to

---

[257] The story of the cave in Plato's Republic
[258] Rabindranath Tagore (1861-1941) was an Indian poet, philosopher, and Nobel laureate, who tried to deepen mutual Indian and Western cultural understanding.

experience an illusion is to react to something that isn't. If your world is a simple effect of an error of thought, your search for meaning, completion, bliss, will not be found there. And meaningful solutions to your problems will not be found at the level of interaction between bodies. They are to be found in the mind.

Your faulty thought process is the cause of your sense of self-deprivation. Do you need guidance through? If you do, where is *helpful guidance* to be found in the midst of the ever-changing? It is true that when the student is ready, the teacher appears.

Nowhere Man ... don't worry
Take your time ... don't hurry
Leave it all ... Till somebody else lends you a hand

Lennon & McCartney
Nowhere Man

Summary
Ego breaks down to separate because harmony is a threat to its existence. Meaning is whole without contradiction. It is not found by breaking down what you perceive into small, disconnected parts. To break down and analyze is the denial of meaning.

The existentialists along with the sophists and nihilists may have accurately perceived the world as an ever-changing paradox of mixed messages; messages subject to opinions of nothingness, and that a pragmatic social order with an ethics of right and wrong can't be defended, only assumed. However, an ideology of nothingness within the duality of a split mind validates nothingness as a "something" to be transcended.[259] If there is only nothingness, then any idea of objective "truth" is error ... and in the light of nothingness error is not real, only perceived ... making reality not yours to select.

There is something grander than your intellectual world of little beliefs, thoughts, fictions and dreams of nothingness that you made real. Reality is not yours to select.

> *He's a real Nowhere Man*
> *Sitting in his Nowhere Land*
> *Making all his Nowhere Plans*
> *For Nobody*

> Lennon & McCartney
> Nowhere Man

---

[259] *The Way Home p192*

2. What the discipline called Philosophy demonstrates

There are more things in heaven and earth, Horatio, than are dreamt of in your philosophy.

William Shakespeare

Introduction

There are no facts, only interpretations

Friedrich Nietzsche

The discipline of philosophy demonstrates that it is the nature of perception or "to perceive" that brings your mind into the area of uncertainty. And yet, you constantly rely on your perception to try to find solutions to the uncertainty that perception has caused.

Perception

In one of my classes there was a parent advocating for the need to educate our children earlier about the "evils" of alcohol and drug addiction so "our children could have the tools to make informed decisions." Another parent in the same class advocated the need to delay educating our children about alcohol and drugs because within the early educational introduction to the topic, she believed her child became curious to experiment at an earlier age. This is a "damned if you do and damned if you don't" conversation. If you generalize this one example you will see the principle of what your perception of the world of form offers in all areas of experiencing life's uncertainty. Because of the nature of perception, to assess anything and involves the exceptions and contradictions of "damned if you do and damned if you don't" scenarios. This is what makes the dualistic battle of politics, education, economics, ethics, etc., seem like a real life headache. With the throng of exceptions *always* on the level of form, it is time to comprehend the fact that truth is not to be found on this level.

It is self-deception to think that meaningful solutions to the problems in the world are to be found at the level of interaction between individual bodies.

Perception splits details into more details to analyze more details. It says the world is a complex place of many problems. However, because complexity of form does not imply complexity in content, solutions are simple ... except to the mind that perceives uncertainty. There is a complication of resulting data that makes it difficult to see its nothingness. Reality is not yours to select. The discipline of philosophy demonstrates this! *Given the data, how do you explain your denial of the obvious?*

Ah Lord, you pay the price
With the spin of the wheel with the roll of the dice
Ah yea, you pay a fare
If you don't know where you're going
Any road will take you there

George Harrison
Any Road

Being

Your sense of failure is merely a mistake in what you think you are

The complicated contradictions that personality and developmental theorists present will not lead you to understand who or what you are. And if you are not sure about yourself, how can you know your world around you? And if you are unsure about your world-view, what can you use from it to help you find you? You are wrong about the world because you are wrong about yourself. When is enough data enough to tell you that being wrong about what the world is about, is a *direct reflection* of being wrong about you? Either God is insane because the world of his creation does not make sense or "You" as a creation of "Being," have nothing to do with the world. As an effect, the world is your projection of a confused mind, an insane contradiction of a world untrue.

The *Sophists* would say "because perception brings your mind into the arena of uncertainty you cannot know anything including yourself for sure in the ever-changing." *Religious Absolutists* argue for a "leap of faith" to believe in the magical thinking of a god whose creation of good and evil strives against itself. The *Existentialists* ask "From such a twisted reference point, what grounding can you find that makes any sense?" The *Rational Pragmatist* would say "What makes sense is that which is practical." But what is practical is ever-changing. The *Utilitarian Economic Politician* would say "That which makes the most sense is that which serves the many." The *Cosmological Technologist* might throw you a bone by suggesting "We might be able to find out about ourselves, our origins, out there, somewhere beyond the stars." The *Environmentalist* would argue: "How could we consider anything but Mother Earth first when your body is part of Mother?" However, they are all looking in the wrong place. If Rene Descartes'[260] premise "I think therefore I am" is turned around, then "Being" precedes thinking and reality is not yours to select because it already "IS."

Blaise Pascal stated that a systematic philosophy that presumes to explain God and humanity is a form of pride. Within the vacuum of religious nonsense Heidegger[261] became concerned with what he considered the essential philosophical question: What is it, to be? This led to the question of what kind of "being" human beings are. We are, he said, "thrown" into a world that we have not made but that consists of potentially useful things, including cultural as well as natural objects.

Either you are causeless being with no direction or home or you are an effect of a greater cause. If you are an effect, of who or what are you an effect of ... which would also make reality not yours to select.

---

[260] Descartes determined to hold nothing true until he had established grounds for believing it true. The single sure fact from which his investigations began was expressed by him in the famous Latin words Cogito, ergo sum, "I think, therefore I am." From this postulate that a clear consciousness of his thinking proved his own existence, he argued the existence of God.

[261] Martin Heidegger was an assistant to Edmund Husserl, the founder of phenomenology. Besides Husserl, Heidegger was especially influenced by pre-Socratic philosophy (the Sophists), Kierkegaard and Nietzsche.

Value

All things are subject to interpretation; whichever interpretation prevails at a given time is a function of power and not truth.

Friedrich Nietzsche

If all seeing starts with the perceiver, then it is you who judges what is true and what is false. No matter how much you want to believe there is an external objective absolute standard for truth, it is you who decides what standard will be the measure of truth. And if you do not know the "you" that you are, the outcome for the measure of truth will be your confusion played out as an absolutist religious ideology of sacred rituals and/or situation ethics. Reality seems to be yours to select.

The study of ethics is a vague generalization of deciding what is deviant and what is socially acceptable given an ever-changing social context that makes it all gray. This is what William James's pragmatic ethics of situations are all about, not believing that a single absolute idea of goodness or justice exists, but rather that these concepts are changeable and depend on the context in which they are being discussed. How bad, bad is, always depends ... based on the context and decided according to the whims of the court. Degrees of deviancy and intelligence are scientifically measured through questionnaires that show you where you fall on the bell shaped curve of generally accepted norms. Reality seems to be yours to select.

There is an experience of "Being" beyond your perception. There is a value that you already are beyond your conception of what you think value means. That is why reality is not yours to select.

"Everybody's Got One"

I am he as you are he as you are me and we are all together ... Everybody's got one

Lennon & McCartney
I Am the Walrus

Everyone has a set of beliefs or ideology as a way to understand how their world works.[262] These are what "fictions" useful or not are all about. In the world of western philosophy, one system after another has been built upon to unearth an understanding of how the world works; to justify their experience of their world. Because selective perception only selects those witnesses that will demonstrate your system of thought to be true, your ideology is a way to structure your world-view in a way that limits you to the validity of that structure. In other words you will select only that which demonstrates that your beliefs are true. That is because all systems of thought defend their system by excluding that which would contradict it. You have to exclude the exceptions in order to think you can find reasoning in the absurdity of a contradiction you call the world. How else could one judge another group of people by appearances except by

---

[262] This book has a point of view ... to be transcended. *The Way Home p178*

excluding the information that would show them that they are like you!

Although we are some 350 years out of the gate of "The Age of Enlightenment," ideological prejudices based on culture, race, color of skin, sex, religion, intellectual achievement, success, etc., abound. The evolution of our species has made tremendous gains in technology and body comfort, but not in awareness. In the light of what history teaches, each of us makes individual gains of awareness from birth onward, but we are unable to learn from a collective consciousness from out of the past. That history teaches us that we don't learn from history is our overwhelming teacher in the face of our denial. If you honestly take a look at the data, you will see that your own personal history of trials, errors, misconceptions and prejudices are demonstrations of not being sure of what it is you are looking at. Based on this, how could you even consider having a working ideology of the world?

You cannot transcend your ideology
When you think your ideology is the truth

Prejudice will always be as long as you perceive yourself as different. Because YOU ARE ONE CREATION beyond dualistic thinking, beyond perception, beyond form, to honor differences is a breeding ground for misunderstanding. But for those who protest for individuality in denial of their ego insecurity, this is too much to bear. On the level of form *everyone* appears different. What is there to honor ... but magical thoughts and behaviors that honor the appearance of differences? Because complexity of form does not imply complexity of content, form is to be transcended if you are to rise above ideological differences. There is an experience shared as one beyond the intellectual and ideological debates of religion, economics, culture and politics. But it is experienced as shared, not known intellectually.[263]

Now I wish I could write you a melody so plain
That could hold you dear lady from going insane
That could ease you and cool you and cease the pain
Of your useless and pointless knowledge

Bob Dylan
Tombstone Blues

The Making of an Ideology

A crisis is when your karma stomps all over your ideology

Judgment always rests in the past, for past experience is the basis on which you judge. Without a past as a reference point you would not attempt to judge because it would be apparent to you that you do not understand what anything means. This scares you because your ego believes that without your ability to judge, to make sense out of the ever-changing, all would be chaos. About the ever-changing, the ego is correct. Through its eyes as your guide, all is chaos. Nietzsche stated that *"When we find out that the world does not possess the objective value or meaning that we want it to have or have long since believed it to have, we find ourselves in a crisis."* However,

---

without the ego ... all would be your experience of love.

Out of fear of not understanding what you look upon, social conditioning (stabilizing perceptions of beliefs, associations, and rules) is an adjustment to make sense out of chaos. These adjustments are the basis for the making of ideologies; "fictions" as to how you think the world works or should work. There are many different and conflicting ideologies of ego alliances for survival. The simple fact that perception brings your mind into the arena of uncertainty is the reason that the ever-changing fiction is at best negotiated ... or fearfully fought over.[264] "I need to defend my sacred beliefs to fight off the doubt that my beliefs foster" is every ideology's hidden dilemma.

The more complex the ideology the more obscure it is. This enables an ideology to hide the fallacy of its logic. It is a house of cards with no basis for its existence. Its existence is based on a tense (the past) to secure a prediction of a future tense that will never be. For example, the fiction that you are a product of social conditioning and heredity only survives because you have been conditioned to see outcomes as linked to innumerably complex causes that are inconclusive as cause and effect correlations. Another example, if sin (from the past) is real, than retribution or punishment will happen (the future). However, if there is no past there is no sin. If there is no sin, then there is no retribution to come.

---

[264] This is the making of history.

Any present moment you choose frees you from your ideological beliefs that limit you from the expression of your Creative Self.[265]

Evolving?

Nietzsche asserted that the scientific assumption of an orderly universe is for the most part ... a useful fiction

Theorists speculate that the universe started from energy smaller than an atom, and in an instant, exploded into *a projection* of energy evolving to matter and still evolving. Was there a thought behind this energy smaller than an atom? Theistic Evolutionists[266] would say yes. However, the concept of theistic evolution is unnecessary.

Evolving? Everything is evolving constantly into what? Our surroundings around us are so very different than they were twenty five hundred years ago. It is so different than it was twenty-five years ago. We have amazing technology for the exchange of communication like nothing before yet confusion and miss-communication abound. Why? We have been to the moon and back numerous times yet we travel in vehicles in danger of an accident and death. Why? We have an economy that supplies abundance of more than enough for everyone yet we still have scarcity for many. Why? We have an economic market of roller coaster confidence based on who knows what? We have an amazing dissemination of information like never before and are fraught with data

---

[265] *Symbols of Power p131*
[266] *The Way Home p128*

theft, addictions, oppression, violence, suicide and ignorance. Why? What significance has occurred through the history of time?

Evolution is an illusion of conditioned thinking. To see progress in the ever-changing spin is self-deception.

Because everything is in a constant state of change, to survive its "fiction," the old ideology grasps on to the idea of evolving into a process of becoming to explain in a meaningful way the random successive approximations of ever-changing nothingness. Darwin's theory that all forms of life develop through a slow-working process of natural selection is a clever way to describe change as having a purposeful teleology. What natural selection really describes in colorfully fanciful ways are ever-changing forms that change in colorfully fanciful ways

NEWS FLASH: Newspaper heading chosen randomly on May 3rd, 2013; *"Suicide rate spikes among boomers. Suicide rates among middle-aged Americans have risen sharply in the past decade, prompting concerns that a generation of baby boomers who have faced years of economic worry and easy access to prescription painkillers may be particularly vulnerable to self-inflicted harm. More people now die of suicide than in car accidents, said the Center for Disease Control and Prevention ... "* Further down, the article says *"The reasons for suicide are often complex, and officials and researchers acknowledge that no one can explain with certainty what is behind the rise. CDC officials cited a number of possible explanations.*[267]

Over and over again we are inundated with meaningless inconclusive data that complicate and then attempt to explain ever-changing information so it becomes difficult for you to see its nothingness.

Same newspaper: *"Bee die-off is linked to many causes. But researchers stop short of proposing pesticide bans."*[268]
Same newspaper: *"A Spire Caps Icon's Rebirth From Ashes. New York celebrates final stage of World Trade Center's restoration."*[269]

If you look in the newspaper, listen to the news or look around your personal world, there is always DRAMA. Everything is always changing. "We must be evolving into something better" you assess. You are not evolving, just describing the ever-changing through *a self-deceptive magical hope* of smoke and mirrors. Your inability to see change for what it is, is a witness to you not knowing what you are. This makes your unwillingness to see self-deception as your primary problem. Appearances are deceiving because they are appearances. Constantly looking for stability in a place it will never be found demonstrates how lost you are in an ideology you don't even know you have. Your world is not a place to find

---

[267] Tara Parker-Pope / New York Times
[268] Josephine Marcotty / Star Tribune
[269] Meghan Barr / Associated Press

meaning because it was made so you could not escape from your problems.[270]

I am deceived by "nothing" in a form I desire

The existentialists say that if you are evolving, what can you know definitively about yourself? Can you know your world around you if in honesty are evolving into something you do not know? Your problems in life witness to a fact that you really do not know the "you" that you are. Given the data, how do you explain your continued denial of the obvious? Because reality is not yours to select, there is a transcendence that involves an awakening rather than evolving.

Outcomes

You are not experiencing a world ... out there
You are experiencing the conflict of a split mind
Projected as ... out there

John Locke says you are born with a "blank slate." Empirically minded psychologists say that "you" are the accumulation of cultural, social and developmental influences. Because there are so many exceptions that these influences can't explain as to why you are the way you are, it is time to question this ideology as another meaningless effect of a greater meaningless cause. If just for a moment you could get past your selectively perceived correlations that defend your ideology, you

---

[270] *Symbols of Power p51, 100*

would see clearly how a person turns out based on their upbringing is fraught with massive exceptions that lack consistent empirical predictability. And what do you do with the bizarre disposition of a mind identified with the body of animal instincts?[271] Without the experience of transcendent peace the data makes perfect sense to be an evolving Pagan Existential Taoist.

The Two Irreconcilable Goals

We are not as Heidegger says "thrown." Nor do we appear as a "blank slate." In other words, we are not the random effects of a corrupt world. Our world is the result of an already flawed mind in denial of its projection being played out and experienced over and over again.[272] History overwhelmingly demonstrates that our minds have shortcomings of unawareness. To believe you can make a mistake in the ever-changing is to perceive you as flawed. Through the distortion that any mistake causes, you look in and see the flaw then look out to project the

---

[271] Your body is born to respond, react, defend, procreate and die just like any other animal. This is the basis for the irrelevant nature vs. nurture debate ... a perfect example of the dualistic projection of a split mind.

[272] Though they may disagree on the remedy, and apart from the idea of reincarnation, conservative, liberal and existential theologians call this the original sin. Post liberal theologians as Karl Barth, Reinhold Niebuhr, and Paul Tillich, were unwilling to attribute the transmission of sin to procreation, instead attributing it to an already corrupt society. Even still, procreation and a so-called corrupt society are effects of our dis-relation with our self. This is the metaphor we call "the original sin."

mistake away to avoid the consequence of what that mistake might mean to the perception of a "you" as a flawed being.[273] In denial you retain the mistake through dissociation, which would be the experience of spiritual, social and existential alienation (guilt). You sabotage reconciliation with yourself by holding onto two irreconcilable goals: an eternal vs. temporal identity. Projected as conflict called "a world" you are distracted to look for a solution for your alienation in a place that demonstrates your alienation has been accomplished.

You can't solve your problems by using the same kind of thinking you used when you made them. In other words the world you made out of alienation was made so you could not find a solution. With your denial of your projection and disassociation from the mistake you project, you seem to live with the challenge of maintaining ethical integrity yet always falling short because of guilt. It may be that you would abhor the accusation that you play god while you deny being the maker of your world of conflict. Maker of your dream of "no exit," the world is simply an outcome of your mind split between the eternal and the temporal. You can have neither as long as you try to have both. This is the conflict of a frustrated learner as you try to learn an impossible lesson.

Who Killed God?

It's all metaphor representing something else
What do you want to make it mean?

---

[273] Your attraction to guilt

Metaphorically speaking, Nietzsche got it right. When the committee[274] decided that God made a world that would allow pain and death for his creation, didn't we kill him? When it was written that God out of anger wanted to "smite with a pestilence and dispossess"[275] His chosen because of their disbelief in spite of all the signs He performed, yet to have Moses reason with God to save the people, did we not kill God? When it was decided that blood sacrifices were needed to cleanse human kind from a sinful world we said God made, didn't we kill God? Every time we say: "It must be Gods will when a child dies," do we kill God? Maybe Nietzsche was more prophetic then we want to realize when he said: *"God is dead. God remains dead. And we have killed him. Yet his shadow still looms. How shall we comfort ourselves, the murderers of all murderers?"*

In our attempts to make a god in our image,[276] to explain the complexities of our unexplainable world, we killed God. We killed God by making Him inconsistent, subject to the whims of our prayers.[277] Then when God does not follow through, we are disappointed or mad at Him for what we did. That we use our substitutions in a world of forms to occupy our time for a satisfaction that

---

[274] The First Council of Nicaea; 325 AD. This committee can be metaphorical for anything including the committee you allow to go on in your mind.

[275] Numbers 14:1-20

[276] Anthropomorphism is the attribution of *human characteristics* and qualities to non-human beings, objects, natural, or supernatural phenomena such as God, animals and the forces of nature.

[277] *The Way Home p66-67*

never lasts is a statement that God is irrelevant. Isn't that the same as killing God while providing lip service to the contrary? We make a god irrelevant to "Being" by relegating responsibilities to this god that have nothing to do with a world that demonstrates chaos. Then we can be mad at him for not following through. We make a god in the image of a projected split mind by giving him power to love and save and power to be angry and destroy. Then we are mad at him for being inconsistent. We also use that god to justify our theological ideology of nation, patriotism and war as a way to kill God's creation and wonder about God's mysterious ways. Nietzsche was right. We kill God every day in more subtle and crafty ways than we realize.

To make the ever-changing sacred is to paganize and demonize. There are many gods you make to bargain with in your search for happiness. This is what the Pantheon of the gods is all about.

If all the world of form is ever-changing and all beliefs about the world of change are subject to individual interpretation, then when I look out on the world what am I looking at? My interpretation of something that is ever-changing. And what is that?

Why do you refuse to understand that what you look out upon is beyond your understanding? Given the data, how do you explain your continued denial of the obvious? Complicating the results of information does make it difficult to see its nothingness. Reality is not yours to select.

Beyond Phenomenology[278]

When Descartes turned cause and effect around and said: "I think, therefore I am," he should have said: "I am, and when I think, I need redirection to rethink everything I decided."

The phenomenologists reasoned that we subjectively and therefore individually interpret our perceptions of an external world making it objectively unknowable. One more step beyond the phenomenologists is the suggestion that not only is the external world objectively unknowable; it is the mind's projection. Everything you see to experience as external is the projection from your mind. In denial of your projection,[279] you observe your own projection from a different and *seemingly separate* point of view while another aspect of your split mind observes its projection from a different and *seemingly separate* point of view.[280] Your perception of your projection is interpreted and experienced individually as an external fact. The body being *an idea of separation* exists only in the mind as a way to defend and experience the idea of separation/individuality. Therefore, it is an assumption that your eyes see, your body feels and your

---

[278] Phenomenology (from Greek: phainómenon "that which appears"; and lógos "study") is the philosophical study of the structures of experience and consciousness.

[279] Projection makes perception. All projection involves denial lest you would be aware of your self-deception and stop it. Ego is keen on defending your individual perception right up to the death of your so-called noble and altruistic individuality.

[280] You are the me that I refuse to see in you

brain interprets a world external to it. Albert Einstein stated that, a man *"experiences himself, his thoughts and feelings as something separate from the rest; a kind of optical delusion of his consciousness. This delusion is a kind of prison for us, restricting us to our personal desires ... Not to nourish the delusion but to try to overcome it is the way to reach the attainable measure of peace of mind."* This reexamination challenges everything you think!

Physiology is not the study of your mind. It is the study of your mind's projection of a brain to defend the idea of separation. The study of anything in the world is once removed from knowing "YOU." Science will not find a measurable link between body and mind because there is none.

Maybe the phenomenologist's have the right idea, studying their reflection of the world from the view of acknowledging self as a subjective participant. However, somewhere along the line they come to the same place that the cosmological scientist comes to; arriving just in time to watch the Big Bang.[281] "What's beyond the Big Bang?" they ask. This is the place where the phenomenologist will have to leave their tools of study behind. And the empirical scientists' sacred objects of measurement, the study of brain physiology, of sensation and perception will have to be left behind so you can "go through the eye of the needle."[282]

---

[281] The Big Bang is about division. Division is ever-changing. Making sense out of ever-changing division is what is assumed to be an evolution of progress. And so it is, the scientists often look at complexity of ever-changing forms for a purposeful teleology. Before the Big Bang was singularity, the awareness of oneness prior to the duality of thought, subject and object.

If your body as a "thing in itself" can only be experienced subjectively but not known objectively, any study of "a self" or "self-esteem" through the association of a body identity is a fruitless chase through the portal of time. Times history through the study of philosophy, psychology, sociology, theology, etc., demonstrates that nothing is known for sure. However, reassigning a new task for the body (setting it aside) for the awakening of your mind allows you to see your reflection as Spirit. Set aside all your preconceived ideas so you can have an experience that shows you something other than your world through a body. This is an experience not yours to choose but to accept. Is there anybody out there?

Making Waves

Pools of sorrow, waves of joy
Are drifting through my open mind
Possessing and caressing me

Lennon & McCartney
Across the Universe

Waves that crash upon the rocks are wonderful metaphors for power and conflict; with a brief reprieve of peaceful calm. A boat gliding through waves is another wonderful metaphor for journey, travel, and safe passage. Light waves that travel across the universe is a wonderful metaphor for astral travel[283] and spiritual being. Be

---

[282] Matthew 19:24
[283] *Symbols of Power p57-63*

deceived no more. Other than as a metaphor, do not limit yourself to a concept of light or energy waves

Energy and light are your conceptual experiences of a cosmological orientation. Though they may paint a picture of an experience beyond words, those who cross over and return to tell, do not grapple with these concepts. Magnetic fields of nature appear hidden with measurable effects of polarity, attraction and protection from the sun. These waves may represent spiritual dynamics but they are metaphors. The aura of a body detectable by the discriminating eye is still within the confines of a cosmological orientation; keep moving.

The only way your ephemeral body can detect the spiritual is if the spiritual takes on an ephemeral persona. This is what visitations are all about. Be not deceived. Your direct experience with the spiritual in the world is a projection from your mind. What you think you are experiencing out there in the cosmos of space is coming from within the heart of what you think you are. Be not deceived; keep moving.

> *There's a river that I know*
> *And this river, it just flows*
> *To a place within my heart*
> *Journey's end back to my start*
>
> *But it's not for me to know*
> *What all these things foretold*
> *Written in the days of old*

It's in the last dream
The conscious slip-stream
It's in the last dream

Matt Karayan
The Last Dream

You may think the waves are coming from "out there," but they are not. Think again, reflect! To begin to perceive accurately is to question as real the uncertainty of an "out there." There isn't anybody out there.

Passion

As I have said, "To derive meaning always makes the observer a participant." It is helpful to remember;

For there is nothing good or bad
But thinking makes it so

William Shakespeare
Hamlet; Act 2, scene 2

Nietzsche, Heidegger and Sartre could not wholly negate the irrelevance of an ever-changing world. To posit meaning in the midst of it, they took a *passionate* "leap of faith." For Nietzsche it was a will to power. For Heidegger as a supporter of the Nazi's it was freedom through order.[284] For Sartre it was individual power and

---

[284] Having a pessimistic view of human nature, Heidegger argued that humanity was doomed to conflict and chaos unless controlled by an exterior and overwhelming force. He viewed government primarily as a device for ensuring

freedom to be regained through group revolutionary action. All three views have been misused to justify oppression.

To get past ideology is to find what? Is to negate the irrelevant resisted by what you fear you might find; the canvas of a nihilistic "nothingness." Are you afraid to find the passionate individualism of anarchism[285] that reinforces your fearful need for order?

If the whirlwind is a place of differences, comparisons, the duality of resolution vs. indecision,[286] disagreement, conflict, compromise and confusion, what can you be passionate about? A better question to ask is "can I be passionate about whatever I want to be passionate about and not be invested in the outcome?" And, "if I can, how do I get there?"

A unified goal for peace of mind allows you to see the means to peace while overlooking the exceptions to its accomplishment.[287] If the means to peace can be found in everyone you meet, your ethical dilemmas become

---

collective security. However, his ideology taken to an extreme for order became a justification for totalitarian governments that breed the conflict and chaos he wanted to avoid through order. Later, in private he called his affiliation to Nazism "the biggest stupidity of my life."

[285] Violations do not mean we need more rules. Violations mean the rules don't work. The concept of alienation is an existential tenet played out as violation. Rules don't apply because the primary cause is not addressed.

[286] Hegel's dispassionate dialectic; process philosophy

[287] This is the proper use of selective perception. To overlook the exceptions to its accomplishment is also the proper use of denial.

irrelevant. It is true that you will not always be consistent in your endeavor. Even if you are consistent, someone will see fault. So what, now you have a unified goal for passion that also meets Kant's categorical imperative.[288] Your passion for peace is a unified goal that transcends perceptual uncertainty.

Where do I go for Meaning?

What does the discipline called philosophy demonstrate? The Greek philosopher Heraclitus maintained that all things are in a state of continuous flux, that stability is an illusion. Because you fear what you do not know (and you do not know yourself as you think), to ward off fear, stability becomes security, meaning. However, the ripples of the ever-changing for stability, security, and meaning are confined to interpretations of duality via perception. Because it is the nature of perception or "to perceive" that brings your mind into the area of uncertainty, the ephemeral is a negotiated reality. This makes morality fuzzy and ethics absolutely situational. Any attempt to moralize the temporal order of how people, things and events should behave as an attempt to justify order in the world of your mind will always find its exception. Armies used to instill order have been misused to foster oppression out of fear. Religious wars justify killing in the name of God and country. Hedonism[289] justifies the raping of Mother Earth

---

[288] Kant's *categorical imperative* expressed that no matter how intelligently one acts, the *results* of human actions are subject to accident and circumstance. Therefore, the morality of an act must not be judged by its consequence, but only by its motivation.

for its own comfort. Social consensus based on utilitarian ideals[290] preclude justice for the individual and thus for all. Libertarian views to defend individuality are feared by many as a step short of anarchy. These few examples represent a confused mind's maladaptive attempts to find safety in a place it can't be found. "Where do I go for meaning?" you ask.

Well the deputy walks on hard nails
And the preacher rides a mount
But nothing really matters much
It's doom alone that counts

And the one eyed undertaker
He blows a futile horn
Come in she said I'll give ya'
Shelter from the storm

Bob Dylan
Shelter from the Storm

---

[289] Hedonism is a school of thought that argues that pleasure is the only intrinsic good. In very simple terms, a hedonist strives to maximize net pleasure (pleasure minus pain). Epicureanism is a form of hedonism, insofar as it declares pleasure to be the sole intrinsic good. However, its conception of absence of pain as the greatest pleasure and its advocacy of a simple life make it different from "hedonism" as it is commonly understood.
[290] The term utilitarianism is specifically applied to the ideal that the supreme objective of moral action is the achievement of the greatest happiness for the greatest number.

The concept of equality in the physical world is an *ideal* of justice. It is an ideal because no matter how much and how hard you try to legislate justice, someone will feel violated! How many times have you heard it said, "Life is not fair." And in the name of legislating the language of political correctness there will be a violation of your freedom of speech. You seek for stability in the disciplines of psychology, sociology and education. There is no end to the obsession that more is better when it comes to education for degrees, licenses for control, education for cultural understanding, professional conduct (ad nauseam) and a legislative insanity that breeds the need for regulation and compliance. And so the best we do for ongoing educational certification is a collective dance of regurgitating the same issues masked from awareness through different forms of cultural differences. Limited to a conditioned world-view of dualistic thinking, there is "no exit" from violation. Rather than question a thinking that perpetuates conflict, you continue to specialize, diversify, personify, individualize, maximize, justify and basically complicate your thinking so its nothingness can't be seen. Accuse me of being a pessimist and you complicate the point. With clever platitudes you justify, rationalize and minimize away the point that your problems in the world have to do with faulty thinking. "This is the best we can do" you say or "we have done well with where we have come from" or "don't be so negative" or "be patient, we're evolving" or use a pithy saying "some men see the world the way it is and ask why? I see the world the way it can be and say why not?" Complicating the results of information does make it difficult to see its nothingness. But for some, this is a fear provoking thought. So you ask "where do I go for meaning?"

"Being" Beyond the Dust of Time

All of your thinking is in comparisons and contrasts. Although this seems to make you rich in expression, it is limiting in experience.
And if this is all you know, what I am talking about when I am talking about an experience beyond the expression of your thinking?

"To be" is a concept that points to an experience of "Being." "Being" is your experience beyond any property of matter, polarity, metaphors of spirit, energy, light, nature, God, etc. Used to describe, these metaphors can either help you through the dualistic maze of dust, or delay you into a lull of self-deception.

For example, just like it is a ruse to try to spiritualize the ever-changing by trying to bring God into it, it is also a ruse to try to spiritualize death as "The Great Circle of Life" when all it is, is a symbol for your mistaken mind. However, "The Great Circle of Life" can be used to transcend it altogether! You "Being" beyond the dust of earth and time can use nature and its processes as metaphors to explain your passage beyond nature, as a meaningful experience.[291]

In a world of continuous flux stability is an illusion and meaning is always fleeting. As long as all things are subject to interpretation and whichever interpretation

---

[291] *Symbols of Power p43-52; The Way Home p149-151*

prevails at a given time is a function of power and not truth, there will never be an equality that is universally experienced as self-evident. The story of our history says so. Start holding your thoughts as suspect to self-deception so you can be open to a totally different experience ... an experience beyond your dualistic world-view that holds your thoughts captive.

There is an experience of "Being" that makes "perfect sense" beyond the empirical measures of sensation and perception. There is an experience of "Being" that makes "perfect sense" beyond an intellectually rational logic. There is an experience of "Being" that makes "perfect sense," that does not involve "a leap of faith."[292] There is an experience of "Being" that makes "perfect sense" beyond the instability of the ever-changing.

This is the question that must be asked. Where do I go for meaning? If everything is subject to interpretation and change, and is different in each person's mind, meaning is a collective hunch to be negotiated as something to be agreed upon by the majority. It is to be benevolent for the minority, and just for all. Maybe we were all as if "thrown" here to figure it out. Thrown to figure what out? This is it. There is no meaning but the meaning you make it mean. The idea of morality and ethics is merely a matter to establish a social order, always subject to change.

It is the same for all. There is one fate for the righteous and for the wicked. This is an evil in all that

---

[292] To have faith is to believe because you do not have the emerging experience of you "BEING NOW."

is done under the sun, that there is one fate for all men. Furthermore, the hearts of the sons of men are full of evil, and insanity is in their hearts throughout their lives. Afterwards they go to the dead.

Ecclesiastes 9:2-3
The Preacher

"Appearances are deceiving because they are appearances" is a statement of non-duality. Again, Heraclitus stated that within the ever-changing whirlwind the idea of stability is an illusion. The *Phenomenologists* say the world is an observable occurrence that appears in acts of consciousness. The *Existentialists* expound the idea that the world is the experience of an absurd aberration. The *Nihilists* simply state that the world is essentially meaningless. Because this is a place where meaning cannot be found, ideologies are made to make sense out of nothingness. And the defenses of these ideologies of nothingness are endless. "Where do I look for meaning when none is to be found?" you ask. It is for you to negate the irrelevant so you can start looking in a different place, a place not of your making, where reality is not for you to select.

The world is not a place to find meaning as long as you are following the dictates of the ego. Ego uses the world as a way to deny you meaning. Against a sense of temporary existence that Heraclitus describes, there is an experience of being outside of the intellect. There is a knowing of permanence that once experienced is unshakable. Within this experience you will never again fully believe in the ego's guidance.

Judgment as Impossible

The more I think I know, the less I listen
The more I realize "I do not know," the more I listen

Where do you go for meaning when perception believed to be able to bring you certainty actually brings your mind into the arena of uncertainty? To not know "you" engenders fear. Judging, weighing, measuring, comparing, for meaning is how you compensate for a solution to ward off this uncertainty. But if you are not anything ephemeral, what you are doing is sampling oranges to see what an apple tastes like ... over and over again. It is true that you make decisions when to cross a street. However, judging your world for meaning has not been your best asset. In fact, it's been your liability. History teaches that we are no closer to knowing ourselves or our world through judgments.

Descartes' made the comment "I think therefore I am." Erroneously Descartes' put the cart before the horse. Instead, he should have said, "I am, and when I think, I confuse myself."

Of course you do not know what you are looking at. How could you, you don't know what you are. And yet you persist in trying to solve problems by using the same kind of thinking you used to create them. Trying to use a world you don't understand as an indication of what you are or should be is your whole self-esteem dilemma.[293] Of

---

[293] In the world of psychology people try to build a self-esteem

course this reasoning is circular and self-defeating. But that is not the point. The point is that you do not understand the depth of your denial!

That is why *judgment is impossible.* You might say, "now wait a minute, I judge all the time!" Do you? When you judge, you select, label, qualify and separate. Because reality is not yours to select, you have done nothing to interfere with reality. You merely added things to your picture that gives you colors to your experience of your projection. You make choices of good and bad, right and wrong, beautiful and ugly, etc., as preferences that have nothing to do with reality. This is not judging as much as it is an exercise of futility to deny that appearances are deceiving because they are appearances. Your attempt to establish any kind of meaning out of the ever-changing of movement and noise is not judgment. It's deciding how the deck chairs should be arranged on the maiden voyage of the RMS[294] Titanic. How do you judge or make static sense out of process? If it is not your role to judge and history demonstrates a strong case for this, you are involved in an exercise of futility you call "judging."

Overlooking nothingness is to judge correctly

Things are labeled insane when they don't make sense. There is *a direct correlation* trying to make sense out of what can never make sense and your experience of frustration, depression, anger, guilt, loss and fear. And

---

(whatever that is) out of a world they can't understand when the self they don't know, made a world they don't understand; how truly insane.

[294] Stands for Royal Mail Ship

this makes empirical sense! Given the data, how do you explain your continued denial of the obvious? Freud would say that there is an unconscious guilt that would explain your resistance of the obvious.

Your deception to think you perceive accurately is a clear indication that you believe reality is yours to select. However, there is an experience of "being" beyond the uncertainty of perception's reality unknown to you until you experience it. The relinquishing of judgment is the way to get out of the way.

Stop trying to decide who you are
So who you are can tell you

Decision

The power of decision is yours. Not as the world decides when it comes to theories of personality development, codes of ethics, ideologies of politics and economics, theologies about God and what to decide between paper and plastic in the checkout lane. If your mind is split in a battle between the eternal and the temporal, your battleground is in your mind, not in its effect you call a world. Because it is your mind that gives your world meaning, the world has nothing to do with meaning. Everything your world represents is a projection that testifies to your minds battle. There is no overlap or compromise in this because the eternal and the temporal cannot be reconciled. To choose the temporal is to choose the duality of a split mind. Here your choices become an endless maze of more choices. To choose the eternal is the unity of no opposition. To choose to value the temporal is to give your power to nothing. Thus you give up your opportunity to learn that nothing has no power over you.

The mark of a moderate man is freedom from his own ideas. Nothing is impossible to him because he has let go.

Tao Te Ching #59

If you look honestly at the data you will find that it is the nature of perception or "to perceive" that brings your mind into the area of uncertainty.[295] Because you are uncertain you collect data to find certainty. And yet, in the midst of all this complex data for understanding, understanding eludes human kind. The greatest minds of our history; the Existentialists, Sophists, Anarchists, Nihilists, Phenomenologist's, Pragmatists, Empirical Scientists and Rationalists are correct in thinking "there is no real order, just a collective hunch out of uncertain ever-changing perceptions." This explains why ethics is always situational. However, there is a single simple content that brings understanding to complexity.

What the Research from this Book Suggests
The history of what philosophy says indicates that:

1) The world is a preoccupation of one problem after another.
2) The world is a closed system, a set-up so meaningful solutions cannot be found within it. In other

---

[295] Yes I know, among other things I've said this over and over again. *Symbols of Power p24, 29; The Way Home p171*

words, to measure anything in an ever-changing world for meaning through the perception of an uncertain mind, with the collection of imprecise data, will lend itself to the conclusion of ambiguous meanings.

These two points are consistently reliable. Your refusal to recognize this becomes an obstacle to your learning progress, making you vulnerable to being preoccupied with diversionary tactics such as *complicating the results of information to make it difficult to see its nothingness.* As a student you would be frustrated, trying to learn impossible lessons such as where in the world can you find purpose, contentment and esteem. The ego will always give you little elusive pieces of a pie of nothingness to chase after, to keep you from looking within.

A decision to focus beyond your experience of the everyday would have to be purposeful and redirected. This is needed because not everything you have been trying to learn has value to you. *Negating the irrelevant* allows your creative mind[296] room to look for "you" beyond any ideology. If your goal is one that unifies your mind to look beyond *complicating results of information that make it difficult to see its nothingness,* you will have a different experience than what you have gotten lost in.

I need to stop deciding who I am so who I am can tell me

---

[296] *Symbols of Power p131-159*

First Principles

The opposite of what the world teaches is that the relinquishment of judgment is the way to get out of the way.[297] *This involves a fundamental shift about everything you've decided.*

To rise above the complex paradoxes of the social order of the ever-changing for a meaningful understanding of what is going on, would be to think in principle. Because life is a series of events fraught with a perception of exceptions, contradictions, absurdities and self-deception, a sociology, philosophy, psychology and theology that could clarify *primary motivation* for all behaviors would simplify matters. For example, a non-dualistic unified goal towards peace would be,

Everyone is always doing one of two things
They are either calling for help or extending love

I fully realize this is unbelievably simplistic in approach. But as a unified goal for peace of mind, it is not difficult for the disciplined mind to apply. *All consistent applications have their experience.* Look within. Isn't all you are about either a call for help or an extension of love? You know this is true for everyone you meet when you see it in you. You know it is true for you when you see it in everyone you meet. Inclusiveness negates the belief in exclusiveness that separates. It also diffuses the need to make all the judgments of comparison the world seems

---

[297] *Symbols of Power p15, 16*

to offer. Inclusiveness diffuses all the prejudices that the appearance of differences seems to offer.[298] *All consistent applications have their experience.*

The discipline called philosophy clearly teaches that the complicating of the results of information has only confused your ability to see the nothingness of all the information generated.

Since your impulse is to perceive and judge what you do not know and not know that you do not know, the practice of consistent application regarding this principle is a practical way to move beyond your temptation to want to judge ... your only block to peace of mind. Said another way,

My function is to only decide that I do not know what is best for me, in recognition that I do not know.

Moving towards consistent application is to move towards allowing for no exception to the principle at hand. This work becomes easier when you recognize that your mind is basically out of control.[299] Don't make the mistake of trying to make yourself an exception to the existential masses. Your experience of a world of conflict is a projection that testifies to the fact that you are confused about yourself. Again, this makes judgment impossible.

---

[298] I am not saying to put yourself in harm's way as far as a body goes. I am saying that ignorance rules the world and it is a good idea to get out of the way.

[299] I don't mean this as an insult. I mean it as a matter of fact.

Through a clearly focused goal for peace of mind, you can use your liability of projecting a split mind as an opportunity to heal it.

To be free of conflict requires only one thing: A goal that is not itself conflicted. Trying to change anything is a form of battle; wanting something that can only be ours in the future is to block our potential to be happy now. Therefore, set for yourself a goal that can be fulfilled where you stand. Make this instant your door to freedom and you will find that it will crack open a little further each time you return to this moment in peace.

Gerald G. Jampolsky
Teach Only Love

Conclusion

"Gentlemen" he said, "I don't need your organization.
I've shined your shoes; I've moved your mountains and marked your cards.
But Eden is burning. Either get ready for elimination.
Or else your hearts must have the courage for the changing of the guards."

Bob Dylan
Changing of the Guards

Nowhere man, what about the world you see? Is there anything about it you can rely on? The roads you follow, where do they lead you? They lead you to the signpost that says "nowhere in particular."[300] And after you get there, then what? The cities you build crumble with time. Science has saved you from what? The world you see has disappointed you over and over again. In the light of situation ethics, what is the truth?

> *As an aspect of my mind*
> *Together we walk in time*
> *Upon a thousand trails it seems*
> *'Till we waken from the dream*

Matt Karayan
The Last Dream

You do not have to believe any of the conclusions this book has to offer. However, I do not know where you will go in the ever-changing to find your bliss. Maybe a compromise is in order; that bliss is but an imagined pie in the sky concept that is as fleeting as the wind and rain. My approach in this quest was to negate the irrelevant[301] so what is relevant would be self-revealing. What the discipline called philosophy teaches is that:

1) The world is a matter of arbitrated thoughts, the negotiation of selective perception. In that place there is no truth to know.

2) Change as "Becoming" is a conditioned view, an illusion that you are evolving.

---

[300] The signpost on the cover of the book *The Way Home*
[301] That which is immaterial or beside the point; mindless distractions

3) Either truth precedes perception or nothing makes sense.

4) If truth precedes perception, reality is not yours to select.

5) Therefore, what "you are" is not yours to decide.

6) Because you are not evolving, you are not lost to the ephemeral dust of existential nothingness. "You Are" changeless; not yours to decide what you are.

And once again as you look upon the world, does it occur to you that you have gotten lost in the insanity of your own perception of perpetual uncertainty? Do you see shadows of what is not there and hear meaningless echoes that make no sense? Do you not know this because you have been too busy giving meaning to everything you think you see? Have you reacted out of a fear of not knowing what you are by clinging to relationships you say are out of love ... when they are out of fear, in the name of love? Do you know what love is if you don't know the you, you are to love? It may be that love can heal all wounds but love does not cause the wounds that it heals; never! Did you set yourself up to grieve the loss of a loved one that was never yours to possess and then think love hurts when it is guilt and fear that causes all your pain? Is your communication problem with another but a reaction to your perception of the insanity you hold dear? Do you actually communicate with no one, isolated from reality and alone in your universe? Is there anyone out there?

I hear echoes whisper, about issues of control
But don't you know you got to be asleep
When you talk as if you know
Isn't it funny, how easy we debate about anything
When the river flows from the mountain top
Right back into the sea

Matt Karayan
Shine Your Light

Over-looking reality, do you only see your split mind and wonder why you experience conflict over and over again? Is there a Spirit of Truth quietly calling you home but you do not hear its call because you are preoccupied in your projecting mind playing your drama story? Your story line is a fiction you are playing over and over again, trying to figure it out. What part of your world makes any sense? Do you need to rethink everything so you can begin to move beyond thinking all together?

What the discipline called philosophy teaches you when you negate the irrelevant is that reality is not yours to select.

Milk the cows of gladness, before they all go dry
Search the rim of madness, before you learn and sigh
Become a parch of dryness, before you stop to drink
Ascend the arch of whyness before you try to think

James Seals
Cows of Gladness

3. Principles of Orientation

A. The Laws of Chaos
B. First Principles
C. Principles of Being
D. Principles of Mind

A. The Laws of Chaos[302]

Because all seeing starts with the perceiver
And perception brings your mind into uncertainty
Laws are attempts to give a semblance of order to chaos

1. What "a thing is," is always changing.

Matter exhibits patterns of predictability[303] as observed by earth's cycle. However, this cycle moves within parameters of continuous disintegration and regeneration. Because matter is in a constant state of flux,[304] what "a thing is," is always changing and therefore;

a) Nothing exactly repeats itself
b) No two things are exactly alike
c) All things are fleeting
d) And therefore, can only appear to be[305]

Because projection makes perception, the concept of change as reality only exists as perceived through a duality of thought.

---

[302] "The Laws of Chaos" is a contradiction in terms
[303] A "continuous randomization of successive approximations" *Symbols of Power p44*
[304] Heraclitus
[305] Plato's cave of shadows that are mistaken as real.

2. Any concept of an eternal reality cannot be derived from change.

The concepts of an absolute and of change are two different ways of looking. Because no concept of an absolute can be derived from change, those who invest in change as their experience of meaning will block their ability to experience the absolute.[306]

3. Acceptance of the eternal and the temporary is impossible.

Because acceptance of the eternal and the temporary is impossible, trying to make them coexist can only be done through the magic of dissociation. That your left hand does not know what your right hand is doing is an example of disassociation. Your disassociation from your remembrance of the eternal projected as a split mind is what the absurd chaos of the world looks like. The magic of dissociation is your erroneous attempt to spiritualize the temporal. That an eternal God is involved in a material temporal is your attempt to spiritualize[307] the temporal. The use of metaphors to direct you beyond the temporal is something else.

4. Rules are an attempt to bring order to chaos.

Rules are not made to be broken. Rules are made to bring meaning and order to chaos. This demonstrates and

---

[306] This is the atheistic existentialists' dilemma of throwing the baby out with the bathwater. They may be correct about the dirty bathwater of a meaningless world, but their focus on the dirty bathwater cost's them their ability to experience the obvious baby ... of transcendent peace.

[307] Or make sacred

hides the fact that your world of uncertain perceptions makes no sense at all. Rules are broken because they cannot bring order to chaos. Who among us do not break rules? Only an underlying tension of misplaced anger, guilt and fear can result.

5. All energy forms, light waves, vibrations, magnetic fields, auras, etc., are properties of matter.

Space tells matter how to move
And matter tells space how to curve

Albert Einstein[308]

The distance light travels in one second is not constant. On a spectrum, light takes on different forms of matter and can be influenced by other bodies of gravity. Light is not a constant but is dependent on or influenced by:

a)   Its source; which dictates the constitution of its essence
b)   Its field of travel; which has an influence on and is influenced to bend by other bodies, as well as change speed, colors, vibration and sound
c)   Its goal of attraction; which *implies* the idea of purpose (teleology)[309]

---

[308] Einstein is best known as the creator of the special and general theories of relativity and for his hypothesis concerning the particle nature of light. Einstein was a proponent of the *uncertainty principle,* which states that precision in measuring processes is limited.
[309]   In   philosophy,   teleology   (Greek   telos,   "end";   logos,

To understand the concept of light without spiritualizing it would be to see it as a property of matter that obeys the *Laws of Chaos.* Light is not constant. Light like matter does not have a purposeful teleology. But it can be used metaphorically to reflect something else.

Are your beliefs about the world a foundation built on sacred sand? What does the data suggest?

"discourse") is the science or doctrine that attempts to explain the universe in terms of ends or final causes.

B. First Principles

1. First principles cannot be proven. They are experienced.

First principles cannot be proven because they are beyond the empiricism of sense perception.[310] There is a stream of creative consciousness that you cannot think yourself into. But you can experience "the knowing" of these principles[311] directly when you meet the conditions necessary for "knowing."[312]

2. To deny a principle of reality does not make it untrue.

It's just beyond your awareness of experience. Denial is your block to experiencing first principles. For example, you will deny yourself the experience of the present tense when your mind is lost to the experience of the past and the future, but that does not negate the present. Also, hate, anger and fear as blocks to love's awareness does not negate love as much as it blocks your awareness of loves expression.

---

[310] Your experience of an external world

[311] What is a first principle? It is an experience beyond the dualistic illustration of words. The closest it can get to expression is through metaphors.

[312] You will find examples of the experience of First Principles in the following two sections; Principles of Being & Principles of Mind.

3. Deriving meaning out of any observation makes the observer a participant.

The use of "quantitative data"[313] to make base line qualitative comparisons makes every empirical method of study "a leap of faith." In other words, to measure, compare and then evaluate what the data "may suggest" *presumes a value dependent upon the observer.* The world is only real to you because you made it real. You cannot escape this dilemma except through your denial of magical thinking. And that is not escape as much as it is delay.

4. That which is constant is true.

Because all things of the ephemeral are temporary in nature, they are to be considered as fleeting, illusory.[314] Therefore, all things of the ephemeral are not true. The sun may have predictability as to its rising and setting, but is variably imprecise about it. Reset your watch.

5. Sensation and perception have nothing to do with truth.

Sensation and perception only witness to and verify the things of the ephemeral. They bring your mind into the arena of uncertainty[315]

---

[313] Collected bits of discrete information

[314] Deceptive, misleading, erroneous, not real

[315] Plato expressed the idea that by its very nature anything involving perception and change would be imperfect.

6. That which is not real needs the protection of a defense.

The world is not evolving; it's spinning its wheels in the mud. It is repeating the same pattern over and over again in different forms.[316] All your attempts to make ever-changing real are defenses against the truth. The metaphor of smoke and mirrors illustrates the fact that all illusions are protected by not looking at them. That's why the obvious is hard for you to see.

7. All reasoning is circular but not all reasoning is revealing.

To measure validity and reliability factors for any systematic approach by the use of the rules of that system is a closed system limited to the rules of that system alone. In other words, if the rule is that to "know" is to be based on sensation and perception alone then you limit your experience to sensing and perceiving alone. The ephemeral becomes all you will allow for "knowing." Anything that violates the rules of that paradigm, which is an experience other than sensing and perceiving, is to be rejected as irrelevant; an aberration or hallucination of the mind. That doesn't mean the ephemeral is all there is as much as it means that the ephemeral is all there is as experienced through deciding that sensing and perceiving is all there is. Your conclusions may be validating and reliable according to the rules of the game, but the results

---

[316] Though history is obvious in teaches this, you protect yourself from seeing this fact because you fear what it would mean for you to make a fundamental shift in how you view all your investments.

are not necessarily revealing. What is revealing is to see how all this reasoning is self-validating but not revealing.

8. All "so called" objective reality is negotiated.

There are as many points of view as there are people. Because each individual view presumes an individual value, communication (negotiation) is necessary. There is no base line truth in the ephemeral.[317] There is *a collective hunch* we call society, or meaning, or self-esteem, vague enough to remain elusive, according to the consensus of "value."

9. The only place change is meaningful is on the level of the mind.

There is nothing new under the sun. It's just packaged differently. Therefore, to talk about anything on the level of form is to talk about change, differences, conflict, conversations of superficiality; nothing definite. Fundamental change is at the level of mind because it is the only place that determines what the level of form means.[318]

---

[317] Though you may base your decisions on elusive indicators, the primary indicator for the stock market is *your* confidence.

[318] Your lesson is constantly repeated until you find the package (curriculum) that helps you remember what your journey is about. There will be numerous packages to help you along your way. Each one recognized for what it is, is a lesson learned that accelerates your journey through time. Said in other ways, this is your collapse of time, the undoing of karma, the dance of passage.

The world does not make you what you are
You only thought it did
You do not do anything to the world
You were mistaken about what it was for

C. Principles of Being[319]

Wherever you go, you are here

1. "Being" precedes thought.

"Being" is the experience of knowing that precedes thought.[320] Thought is the block to experiencing "Being" because it uses perception as a way to want to know, yet bringing you into the arena of uncertainty. Descartes' Cogito, ergo sum, "I think, therefore I am" has been *presumed* to mean that thought is the necessary cause for knowing "Being." However, "Being" knows "Itself" while thinking removes you from knowing "Being." To perceive your thoughts is the doubt that fears, guesses, believes and presumes etc. Faith becomes potential because it is needed in the realm of uncertainty. Instead of "I think, therefore I am," it is "I Am, and when I think, I believe I am something other than I Am."

2. "Being" is not "becoming" because "Being" already Is.

Because "you" *already are* you are not evolving or becoming. To identify with a world of change through a body of change is to identify with the idea that you are susceptible to change. You spiritualize the world of the ever-changing by believing that it like yourself is

---

[319] Ontology as a division of metaphysics is the study of being. Because it is a field of study, it is once removed from experiencing "Being" directly.
[320] Contrary to Descartes', Nicolai Hartmann argued that reality is prior to thought.

evolving. That is why everything between birth and death seems like real events. However, appearances are deceiving because they are appearances. And what you are not, will not help you understand what you already are.[321]

Transcendence is implied only when the ephemeral is considered. You do not evolve into an awareness of something never to be. Nor do you transcend the ever-changing that is not real. You awaken to the truth of what you already "Are." In the end, the concept of transcendence is just another illusion.[322]

To question Being is to doubt
It assumes a disposition of not knowing
The one who questions is not you because
You already "Are" beyond the experience of doubt

The absurdity of your doubt consumes an enormous
amount of energy because ...
What you are not will not find "You"

3. The experience of" Being" as Known is a quality apart from thinking, sensation and perception.

You experience present thoughts remembered as a past and anticipate an unknown future. That does not mean the present does not exist. You do not examine a number of oranges by tasting, touching, seeing, smelling and hearing to find out what an apple tastes like. You may be lost in process (passage) but what you are is already

---

[321] The Laws of Chaos #2
[322] *The Way Home; P192*

complete. Your unawareness of your completion as "being" does not mean you are not complete. It just means you are unaware of your completion.

4. Because Being "Is," it is always experienced as known "now."

The present tense is the tense of "Being." All thoughts of past and future block your awareness of experiencing "Being" now. *No event has meaning outside of the understanding of any present moment.* All your sickness has to do with your forgetfulness of the present moment.

To search for a self in a place it can't be found
Is to search in a place that isn't
Not in the past, not in the future
Wake up; you're in the present!

To "know you" is to *only* desire to "want to know you now." Let not your thoughts of a past or future teach you what you are not "now."

5. To think is to Dream.

Because you are the Mind of Source, "Being" knows "Itself." To think is an experience other than "Knowing" what "You Are." This is what it means to dream. To not know is the conflict of a mind split between knowing the eternal and perceiving the ephemeral. And your mind cannot do both. Your mind thinks as a substitute for forgetting the experience of "Knowing Being." This consciousness is projected, embodied, limited to and individualized as an ephemeral body. Because your mind experiences a self-imposed limitation, you experience incompletion. This incompletion is the fundamental source of all your motivation to achieve, excel, realize, and find your *bliss* within your self-imposed limits of incompletion. In other words, you have sabotaged yourself to seek and not find. Again, the world was made so you could not find a way out. This is your experience of the tenses of past and future, your linear duality of journey. This is what it means to dream. To those in the process of waking from their dream, this disposition is also understood as passage. Learning becomes an ability you must develop because restlessness reigns when you are lost to your dream.

6.   All psychological, theological and philosophical processes of thinking are helpful if they redirect you to remember your experience of "Being" beyond thought itself.

The defining factor in evaluating anything as being of *value* in the ephemeral is whether or not it helps you to wake up.

> *You dream a dream of a world untrue*
> *Until you can use the dream*
> *To bring you back to you*

7. Remembering your part is in the experience of the Whole.

Being, Self, Source are different ways to verbalize your shared identity within Your Greater Self. Because your mind as split seems to operate as your center of being, you are unaware of your experience of YOU everywhere. Your view of the Whole does not come from your split or individual mind. The understanding of your part comes from the view of the Whole. That is why redirection, guidance to overcome your self-made limits of individuality, is your greatest need. *Relationship is everything!*

8. Spirit is your internal guide that motivates you to remember your journey.

Your experience of the transitory is a fragmentation away from remembering the experience of your shared identity. This fragmentation of forgetting the Self that you share as One is a limitation of thought that allows you the illusion of an individual experience. You cannot know the power "YOU ARE" when you have used the power of your mind to limit you to an ephemeral body. Spirit is your link of communication.[323] It is the meeting place in the world of your mind, split between your identity with "Being" and your experience of your ephemeral dream.[324]

Because of fragmentation, you have limited your awareness of your creative inheritance. Whenever you allow, Spirit uses your experience of a fragmentation you call reality to express your creative Self.[325] Your awareness of Spirit's communication through your so-called individual mind is your breakthrough, your ray of light into the dark, your meditative lesson, your epiphany. It is your reminder of your shared identity with "Being."

---

[323] That still small voice

[324] Some call this the soul concept.

[325] *Symbols of Power 133-159*

Stop deciding who you are
So the Spirit of who you are can tell you

D. Principles of Mind

1. All seeing in the world starts with the perceiver.

What your world means to you is what you make it mean. There is no objective truth through perception. So-called reality is negotiated.

2. Your mind has two ways of looking.

You may think that your mind has innumerable ways of looking but you either "know" directly, or "perceive" which brings your mind into uncertainty. To bring your mind into the arena of uncertainty is to limit. Though you limit, because of uncertainty your choices seem endlessly innumerable. Yet they are all one choice between illusions of conflicting uncertainty. The effect of this limitation is a mind divided in the conflict of trying to serve two masters. Because complexity of form does not imply complexity of content, your choice is simply between "knowing" and the innumerable choices of "perceiving."

3. No thought leaves its source.

Because no thought leaves its source, you always experience the thoughts you choose to entertain. If you seek to limit your mind, you will entertain a world of limits. That is the amazing power of your mind. *Out there* is what you have limited your mind to see. However, because no thought leaves its source, there is no *"out there."*

Because no thought leaves its source you always receive what you first give. The law of karma says: If you give anger, anger you will experience. If you give love, love will be your experience. The question is: "What am I giving to another; for it is this I will give to myself first." What you give will either remind you of peace or be the price you pay to deny you peace of mind. Because no thought leaves its source, do you understand who you are condemning when you judge?

4. Projection makes perception.

Because no thought leaves its source, you do not experience what is out there; you experience what your mind says is out there. That is why your mind always finds what it seeks. If your mind is uncertain about itself, it will find forms of uncertainty seemingly out there to experience doubt. And because projection makes perception, your solution will not be found in your effect (the world of uncertainty) but in the cause, the mind that made the effect real. That is why no solution will be found for you in the world. Your solution is in the mind that made it real.

You will experience your beliefs
But your experience does not make your beliefs true

5. Denial always precedes projection.

Because of denial, you do not know the extent of what you have done to yourself. You project a world out of a split mind as real and experience your internal conflict as externally true. You validate the idea that your mind is correct in seeing a world in conflict while denying that the conflict you see "out there" was made by your mind. Through denial you can maintain the illusion of two separate worlds; an inner world and an outer world.[326] This is why you are your own self-made victim perpetrating your self-made victimization on someone else.[327]

We see the world wrong and say it deceives us

Tagore

The primary effect of limiting your mind is not a world untrue; it is not knowing that you limited it, to make a world untrue. How can you know that you limited your mind when you used the power of your mind to limit it from knowing what you have done?[328] It is this denial that allows you to play out your delusion. That is why you do not understand the extent of what you have done to yourself. This effect is the basis of your need for a unified mind, the unifying goal being peace of mind.

6. Seeing adapts to wish, for sight is always secondary to desire.[329]

In other words, you do not experience the world you see; you experience your interpretation of a world you made to be *out there.* Through perception, beauty, ugliness and justified anger belong to the mind of the beholder. But that does not mean reality is yours to select. In other words,

---

[326] This is how you use the body as a means to deceive you.

[327] The justification for all blame

[328] This is the basis for all circular reasoning as being self-validating but not necessarily revealing.

[329] *A Course in Miracles*

You do not think what you experience
You experience what you think

7. Every effect is consistent with its cause.

Not only do you experience the thoughts you choose to entertain, but those experiences will be consistent *self-validating* representations of their source.[330] If you do not know what you are, you will project that thought as a world unknown to you and not know that you did it. And the world you do not know will be your place to search for a "you" that you are not.

8. Fear is the result of not knowing.

Because every effect is consistent with its cause, the effect of not knowing is a mind divided about the truth of what it is. It is a mind split between knowing and believing. To believe involves perception the arena of uncertainty, expressed through dualistic thinking (split mind). To doubt is to experience the unknown, to dream. To not know engenders fear.

---

[330] That is why empirical data is self-validating but not necessarily revealing. Your conclusion obeys the rules of the paradigm that justified what data would be allowed so your conclusion could be validated as true. All ideologies survive out of selective perception because exceptions to that ideology are intolerable to its survival. It is a closed system of thought that cannot see outside of its thinking. It takes time and enormous energy to try and make sense out of the absurdity of the everyday because of your attempt to make sense out of the senseless you made.

Your fear of the unknown is the fear of a self-made self, projected as the unknown.[331] For you do not know yourself. And to not know engenders fear. This is why your world seems fearful.

Though Descartes' statement "I think therefore I am" was to be a process of systematic thinking to erase doubt through investigation, it actually invited doubt to new levels of systematic insanity. Because your thought processes are about breaking apart, segmenting, dissecting, analyzing, comparing to understand the ever-changing, what you continue to find is never ending questions about the ever-changing. What you find in the realm of thought's uncertainty is never ending effects. To think is the origin of all doubt.

9. To think takes effort.

Knowing is your natural state of mind as abstract. It requires no effort. As a substitute for knowing, *to think* is to question, estimate, judge, assume, imagine, guess, doubt, etc. These aspects of thinking facilitate false experiences, which need defenses of justification through

---

[331] This is the basis for all self-esteem and abandonment issues. It is easy to believe that someone abandoned you when through the denial of your projection and disassociation from this projection, you actually abandoned yourself first. All therapeutic attempts to justify and reinforce the idea of abandonment in your client as coming from the outside are erroneous and self-defeating, leading away from the healing process. Everyone you misperceive as abandoning you has been working out their own journey of misfortune, just like you, until you realize, you "already are" (Principle of Being #2).

self-deception to maintain. Self-deception requires enormous effort to maintain and defend. Your relationships are based on your illusion or fictions of misperception, negotiated against another's illusion of misperception.

The desire to want to know, to learn through doubt, belief and faith along with your defensiveness to maintain self-deception is the battleground of a split mind. And because doubt, belief and faith can also be efforts to maintain self-deception, your need to focus with an open mind[332] becomes essential.

10. Healing is of the mind and for the mind.[333]

To fragment is to divide. To integrate is to heal. Because your mind seeks integration, you cannot serve two masters and have peace of mind. Because the body is part of the ever-changing, the goal of healing cannot be of or for the body. To invest in the body as an end, results in the experience of grieving and death. There are no relationships in this. Rather, it is focus on a divided goal and thus a frustrating self-sabotage. However, what your mind chooses to invest in, it can change its mind about.

11. Peace of Mind is a choice for a unified goal.

A unified goal for mental health would be peace of mind because nothing gives you peace but peace itself ... and the means to peace is peace itself. To choose integration is the journey to transcend the limits of dualistic thinking; beliefs that bring you uncertainty,

---

[332] *The Way Home p53 & 76;* Tao Te Ching #71
[333] *Symbols of Power p22*

conflict and rejection. Healing is the process of integrating your split mind. You may think you are evolving ... until you wake up to peace.

12. Healing that is lasting is attained through peace because *peace of mind* is a unifying goal.

Mind seeks integration. It is your minds natural inclination to achieve harmony through unification.[334] Because minds natural inclination is towards abstraction,[335] "to think" blocks minds natural inclination. This block or interruption is a distraction through many forms[336] that takes enormous effort to maintain. Therefore, healing is a process of choosing to unify a split mind. It is the choices

---

[334] On the level of appearances, this is what drives the individual mind to seek commonality, connection, kinship, society. The whole is *other than* the sum of its parts.

[335] Abstraction (from the Latin *abs*, *away from* and *trahere*, *to draw*) is the process of taking away or removing characteristics from something in order to reduce it to a set of essential characteristics. Negating the irrelevant is a process to take out what you have projected, to reveal what is there or relevant. The mind that connects with the universal flow of creating is beyond boundaries of limitation. These are experiences of an abstract mind. *Symbols of Power p 139-199*

[336] The many forms are a world of limits, regulations, laws, rules, restrictions, boundaries, fences, etc. Given your dilemma of experiencing a world untrue, I do not deny their necessity. Even still, they are all the investments of a world you hold dear to delay your focus for integration. Speaking out of fear, you seem to need boundaries, rules to establish order. Their need demonstrates that the world of your projection is chaos. Those who recognize that they bought the dream, for the sake of convention do time by playing the game.

along your way by which you *sort out* (or negate) that which would conflict with a unified goal. This process of unifying your mind involves the proper use of denial or selective perception to negate or ignore that which would distract you from your goal. *All forms of therapy can be considered as helpful from this point of view.*

Outcomes for peace are experienced as realizations, epiphanies, and statements such as "I never thought about it that way." A realization is not temporary relief; it is release to a larger awareness. It is a collapse in time,[337] a consolidation of what has been learned, or actually unlearned.[338] It is your mind's step towards further integration. It seems to be a process in time ... until you arrive at the place before time ... the place you never left.

The world does not make you what you are
You only thought it did
Nor do you do anything to the world
You were mistaken about what it was for

---

[337] *Symbols of Power p113-118*
[338] negated

4. Miscellaneous Sidewinders

Miscellaneous: varied, mixed, having various qualities, many sided.

Sidewinder: 1) a small desert rattlesnake that moves over shifting sand by looping its body sideways. 2) a hard, swinging blow of the fist, delivered from the side. 3) an air-to-air missile that homes in on a target by a heat-seeking device.

Aphorism: a short or concise statement expressing an observation or general statement of truth.

1985

Cemeteries reflect your belief in separation

*

The one who asks, "Who am I?" Is not you
For if it was YOU, you would not be asking the question
Knowing who YOU already are

1986

The measure of relative quantities by comparing them to
other relative quantities, is the measure of insanity

*

For every black there is a white
Just as for every white there is a black
And within those walls is "no exit" your destiny
Because "no exit" is your goal

*

Are you so busy trying to comprehend everything around
you that you end up understanding nothing?

*

The assumption that the formally educated are more
aware ... is an assumption

*

We build to destroy
Can your despised stupidity save you from your arrogant
cleverness?

*

Intelligence and technology have a direct correlation
Psychological awareness and intelligence do not
Have we out smarted ourselves with clever technology?

*

A rule as an end is a means for restriction
For you will violate it
A rule as a means is an aid for freedom
For you will transcend it

*

Physical comfort has been equated with progress
While progress towards the expansion of your comfort is addictive

*

A paradox is the dis-relation between illusive thoughts of perception

*

A law of justice without mercy is lawlessness

*

Values perpetuate crimes
For it is only a thing of value that is worth stealing

*

A quantitative measure is a meaningless fact
A qualitative measure is the value you decide to make out of that meaningless fact

1987
Your assumption about the intentions of others
Is a witness to your view of your past
Let it pass

*

Like the clouds in the sky
Ever-changing form is formless
Because it is ever-changing

*

*What your mind makes out of its own confusion is the truth
of that confusion*
*Yet, the truth of your confusion is unknown to the confused
mind*

*

*All factors considered, the bell shape curve washes out
Social norms established as rules of conduct make deviants*

*

*That social reform reforms the heart is a lie
That people adjust to the change reform brings is the truth*

1988

*As you go to your workshop to learn about life
Remember, life is a workshop*

*

Any concept of ego does not exist beyond judgment

*

*A child is not socialized to feel anger, guilt or fear
They bring it with them*

*

*Process keeps everything in between
Process keeps everything on the move
Process keeps you on your toes*

*

*From the aspect of your part, the end is not seen
From the view of the whole, it doesn't matter*

*

*The mind of each beholder decides the value of what they
choose to behold
You always respond to what you first valued to behold*

*

In self-deception can ignorance think it is free

Only when you think in terms of process does motion seem to have meaning

*

Your investment in what returns to dust is confusion at its best

*

Learning from your mistakes is not an application of linear thinking
If it were, there would be no repeat violations

*

Addiction is a blind reliance that ignores alternatives
The apparent need for fossil fuel is one of society's justifiable addictions

*

Pleasure and pain are the fleeting conditions of being human
And the incredible lightness of being?
That's something else

*

Not even for the most proficient dream weaver does life in a body have a plot

*

Sex is as fleeting as pleasure and pain
Once you know this, you can enjoy all three

*

Ethics and morality belong to the concept of a body

1989
Within an instant of your hate is a tyrant made

*

A coward is not one who admits they're afraid
A coward is one who denies their fear

Conditioned thinking is what makes the everyday look dramatic

*

How to make The Everyday meaningfully real
A recipe approach:

To make the everyday meaningful, that is to say;
1) *Easy for viewing*
2) *Palatable for tasting*
3) *Gentle for listening*
4) *Aromatic for smelling*
5) *Soft for touching*

Is to make;
1) *A language with concepts*
2) *Agendas with outcomes*
3) *Theories with planned approaches*
4) *Treatments with labels*

In short, to make the everyday meaningfully real involves;
1) *A dash of this*
2) *and a dash of that*

PS - Some words of caution for the unaware:
1) *Be careful to follow the directions very carefully! The wrong combination of ingredients can boil over or be highly combustion-able!*
2) *Even still, you never end with what you intended. Often, the results turn bitter to the taste.*
3) *Therefore, do not attempt to make this recipe without authorized supervision or professional training.*

*

Your life events are random
What you make them mean, looks different
*

If the sanctity of life is the breath of a body, your body will
be your homage of death
In the meantime; the breath of your body is a passing fancy
*

With or without mind's attempt to interfere
All bodies know how to dance with earth, air, fire and
water
*

You made the world so you could participate in what you
made
*

Learning is acquired
Knowing "Self" is beyond learning
*

Your socialization does not admit to fear as your primary
motivator
That would implicate your sacred institutions of education,
business, politics and religion as being ... pointless
*

Fate is a reality of the moment
Not a concept of time
*

Your response to the world of appearances as something
real ... is your unreal experience of an illusion ... just like it
is your illusion of an unreal experience ...

1990
Having a world-view is not important
Being aware of your world view, is

You color the world with the attitude you carry

*

Thoughts are a function of mind, not a reality
That's why you can experience "illusion"

*

History teaches clearly
Whatever was ... will be again
Just packaged differently

*

Because Communism is an ideology to "free the people," it
is as clever, classless and free as capitalism
It's called "point of view"

*

The fruits of desire are pleasures fleeting moments

*

The institution is an imitation
A metaphor for something else

*

What once was a luxury is now a necessity, is the
adaptation of an addictive society

*

A college degree is not a prerequisite for happiness

*

"It was meant to be" is fate's justification
"What happens, happens" is fate's reasoning
What is beyond the concept of fate?

*

You can be educated and unaware
This is called intelligence
You can be uneducated and aware
This is common sense

*

1991

Thought cannot be proven as an entity of existence
Consciousness cannot be a matter of scientific investigation
There is nothing that can be a matter of scientific investigation

*

Each and every effect reflects its source
You are the source of your world
How do you like it?

*

Some symbols, places and rituals of Mother Earth are deemed more sacred than others
However, either it is all sacred, or none of it is

*

Education does not save you from deception
A readiness to listen does

*

Standardized testing is a little of everything and a lot of nothing

*

Are you so informed that you're choking on it?

*

Evolution is the idea of building from one generation to the next
Your effects seem to be a cause for the next generation
Yet, everybody starts over

*

Productive members of society continue to produce society

*

To be fooled is to fool you first and not know it

*

1992

Those who see deception in the world do not see self-deception first

*

Money doesn't bail you out of anything

*

What was once luxury is now necessity
What was once innovative is now commonplace
Everything is continually progressing ... in a circle of smoke and mirrors

*

Oil is one of society's justifiable addictions
Addiction's fruit is either to withdraw
Or choke to death on your justifiable addiction

*

Through a technologic economic consuming vacuum of dependence, we teach our children "empowerment"
How can you ask anyone to reach beyond what they have been trained to need?
Unless true "empowerment" is beyond the mindset of the world's teaching

1993

The world is very tired
Tired of thinking ...
Thinking of what was ...
Thinking of what may be ...
Thinking very hard ...
Thinking over and over again ...
When will the world of thought lie down to die?
When you surrender to the truth within

*

1994

Consciousness is recognized by thought's reflection
What is beyond the duality of this reflection?

*

The color of a word is its meaning
Only personal to you

*

Whenever it is a matter of flux
The outcome is a matter of "It depends"

*

Society is a collective hunch based upon a conditional consensus

*

Lose not the sight of Self wherever you go
Just in case you happen to misplace yourself

1995

Anarchy exemplifies the ultimate in control
It justifies any means to reach its goal

*

The only difference between the evening soaps and the news is that ... The news portrays the spoofs as real

*

Know that you have been easily fooled

1996

The mind is something else ...
The ideas it maintains ...
The scenarios it plays ...

*

To assume the body and make it so, does not make it so
But you will experience depression

*Value in the eye of the beholder
Is only a concept of thought*

*

*Rather than being an eyewitness to appearances of fleeting thoughts
Be a direct witness to that which lies beyond all appearances*

1997

*Wisdom does not see boundaries
Conditioning does*

*

*Boundaries for security and order
Are your body's means for violation*

*

*Beyond the last paradigm is movement and noise
What's beyond movement and noise?*

*

*The new order understands gratitude
The old is accustomed to loss*

*

The concept of intelligence is the most ridiculous concept in the world of your mind

*

You believe because you do not know

1998

You can't change your world from within a cave

*

*Anarchy reigns
But only in the mind that thinks it*

*

1999
Comfort is a state of mind

2000
People who are not honest as a way to avoid interrogation
Invite interrogation into their lives

2001
An honest question does not have an answer in mind

2002
Experience is discrete ... but only to the separate mind

2003
Whatever you label you limit to a measure of comparison

2004
There is no mistaken thought that is any more or less
They are all the same

*   *

Discipline of the body is an exercise of the mind

2005
If nothing is worse than "The Inevitable"
And ... if you accept "The Inevitable"
Even more ... when you embrace it!
You are free of fear

*   *

Acceptance makes "The Inevitable" ... irrelevant

*   *

2006
Because "YOU" are the destination you never left
Your destination to you is not in the future
*

There is a reason for every lie ... and that's the truth of the matter
To be free of the lie is to see the reason and not the lie

2007
The world you see is not complicated
The mind that sees it that way ... is lost in complication

2008
You believe so much because you know so little

2009
You grieve death because you deny the body its place
*

Time is just the memory of cause with a delayed effect

2010
The world is constantly being made out of your beliefs
*

Mind is the most powerful thing in the universe
To experience it directly, beyond thought, is to know the other side
*

It is the human condition to complicate the simple
*

No matter what happens to you in your life
No matter what your genetics are
"You Are"

You are creation
To not know this engenders fear
*

That thoughtless moment of madness is a memory
Through a worm hole ... lost in its own effects
That's what your journey back is all about

2011

Why are you afraid of your world?
Because you are afraid of the power of what you thought
your mind did

2012

To be lost in the whirlwind of the hurricane
Is to forget there is the calm of the eye

2013

Nationalism as a reason for freedom
Has always been a justification for war
*

Trying to figure out world events through religious and
political differences ... is like trying to understand chaos
"What if" holds you hostage to the hypothetical
*

Being born to die and to take it seriously ...
Makes us the most irrational of all the animals

2014

Those who deny reason cannot be conquered by it
*

Rules are made to prevent violations
Violations are caused by rules that are made to prevent violations

*

Before you die, there is always something to do ...
Let it play

2015

As it seems,
You are born at an unscheduled time
You die at an unscheduled time
And no matter how hard you schedule everything in-between ... everything in-between plays itself out ... and right on schedule

*

We wander the world lost
Not knowing that we are

*

An existentialist is one who lives a life of organized chaos

*

Having a funeral in a big cathedral church with lit candles and rituals ... can make you feel like it was endorsed by God!

*

The ethical atheist is a humanist
This is also ... magical thinking

*

To live life on life's terms
Is to live without "fiction"

*

Learning principles of "Being" has nothing to do with intellectual intelligence
It has everything to do with readiness

*

The only mistake in the illusion of it all
Is the one you don't forgive

* * *

Appendix:

News Flash!
A Personal Thought
Tomorrow Never Knows

News Flash!

August 1st 2013: *Three teens are implicated in the killing of an elderly woman in her home for money. One of the teens who apparently orchestrated the robbery was the elderly woman's grandson.*

Are you evolving? Is this just another bizarre isolated case of a legion of separate isolated cases that happen on a daily basis? Do all these seemingly different forms hide a simple single content? Has your selective perception of uncertainty brought you any closer to peace of mind when anger, guilt, depression and fear have just taken on the seduction of seemingly more civilized forms? Are you evolving or just imagining an evolution of progress through the ever-changing smoke and mirror?

It seems that killing on a massive scale is not as pervasive as in the past. Ethnic and religious prejudice seems tempered and technology has increased world communication on a level unthinkable. However, history demonstrates that evolving information is irrelevant to the idea that no matter what the evolving times are you project an image out of guilt to work through your *individual illusion* of evolving. Your projection of guilt has taken more civilized forms. Yet, it was just stated on the world news that there are 45 wars going on in the world at this time. If you are evolving, how come you can't evolve to the place to learn that there is nothing new under the sun? Out of all the things that have changed, the perception of uncertainty still prevails as it did since the time of the Greeks.

Since the beginning of the Age of Enlightenment 350 years ago, human kind has been hopeful about a "New Age" of reason. However, it seems that no matter how enlightened you have become you still do all the things you did before and employ the same superstitious idols you employed with the same denial you had before. I say the same denial because you want to argue that things have gotten better in so many ways. I am not a pessimist that says things are bad or getting worse. That is not the point. I am asking, "Is your ego for survival's sake relentlessly maneuvering, subtly hiding behind the illusion of educational and technological achievements?" There is nothing wrong with creativity and innovation as the world values it; it's just illusion.

In spite of what you think and regardless of your surrounding circumstances, what seems to really matter is what you are ready to learn when you are ready to learn it. There is a picture bigger than the imaginings of all of us. The illusion of social and cultural learning only has selective value when it helps you learn what your present task is to learn. There is something bigger than all the little crafty designs you made up to measure learning accomplishment. You are no closer to peace of mind than your ancestors. Reality is not yours to select. This is what the data suggests. This is what the discipline called philosophy demonstrates.

A Personal Thought

One of my most favorite reads has been Loa Tzu's, *The Tao Te Ching.* What depth of wonder, revelations of truth, paradoxes of being within the ever-changing; "Doing all without doing ..."

And yet, within the yin and yang of it all, seeking balance within the ever-changing is not the way. It is not about the balancing of illusion that helps you through the illusion; it is about forgiving the nothingness you took as real; that is *The Way through.*

It has been said before "Beware of Maya"
But now I say to you: Be not on guard against nothing
Rather, beware of your ability to make the intangible of nothingness seem like something.[339]

My psychological attachment to the allure of wisdom writings is an easy self-deception. It is a way to cling to the body and experience of the ephemeral world. It is a way to make the illusion of the ever-changing ... seem real. It hides my unconscious resistance to the truth of the matter; there is no world!

Therefore, experience your projection, grieve the despair, and forgive yourself for what you have tried to make your projection mean ... and dance. For your projection has nothing at all to do with the Kingdom That You Are.[340]

---

[339] *The Way Home p179*
[340] *The Way Home p49-52*

I wrote a lot of nothing
Just to tell you ...
That what you thought was something
Was actually ... nothing

Tomorrow Never Knows

Turn off your mind, relax, and float down stream
It is not dying ... it is not dying
Lay down all thoughts, surrender to the void
It is shining ... it is shining
That you may see the meaning of within
It is being ... it is being
That love is all and love is everyone
It is knowing ... it is knowing
That ignorance and hate they mourn the dead
It is believing ... It is believing
But listen to the color of your dreams
Is it not living ... is it not living
All play the game "Existence" to the end
  Of the beginning ... Of the beginning
   Of the beginning ... Of the beginning
    Of the beginning ... Of the beginning
     Of the beginning ... Of the beginning
      Of the beginning ... Of the beginning
       Of the beginning ... Of the beginning
        Of the beginning ... Of the beginning

Lennon & McCartney
Tomorrow Never Knows

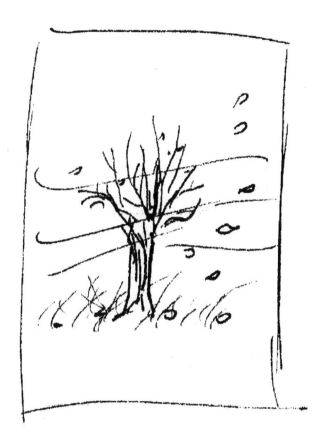

40299217R00160

Made in the USA
San Bernardino, CA
16 October 2016